An American History Lesson and a Wake Up Call for America

By "The Last Angry Man"

Jack B. Walters

Check out article
A Wake up call for America
August 17, 2010

Order this book online at www.trafford.com
or email orders@trafford.com

Most Trafford titles are also available at major online book retailers.

Printed in the United States of America.

ISBN: 978-1-4907-0998-7 (sc)
ISBN: 978-1-4907-0997-0 (e)

Trafford rev. 07/24/2013

www.trafford.com

North America & international
toll-free: 1 888 232 4444 (USA & Canada)
fax: 812 355 4082

Contents

Other Persons

Historical Events

Islam book reports

2010

2011

2012

2013

About the Author

I graduated from the University of Buffalo in 1954. I joined The Firestone Tire & Rubber Co. and worked for Firestone for the next 28 years. I was promoted to the position of Plant Manager for three ever larger plants ending my career at the Des Moines, Iowa plant in 1982.

A few months later, I was invited to be a member of newly elected Governor Terry Branstad's staff as the Director of General Services. I served in that position for 8 years. When my wife died suddenly in Feb., 1991, I resigned and have been retired since that time. Two projects stand out as my favorites. The first was the design and construction of a new $25 million dollar Historical and Library Building. The second was starting and completing 35% of the exterior restoration of the State Capitol Building.

I retired to Tucson 20 years ago. I am an outdoor enthusiast. I belong to the Southern Arizona Hiking Club and just before my 70th birthday I completed the 315 peaks award which at that time was the highest award given. These peaks were within 75 miles of Tucson. Later a new club goal was established at 400 peaks. The distance from Tucson was increased to 100 miles. This added several new mountain ranges. I accomplished this goal just before my 80th birthday in April 2008. I continue to hike but mostly trail hikes as age does take its toll. I still golf once or twice a week. I am convinced I know what to do, the problem is doing it. There is no place I would rather be than on a beautiful golf course.

I started writing in March, 2003 when I purchased my first computer.

My first book, "The Life and Times of Jack B. Walters" was essentially my recollection of important events in my lifetime.

After finishing the story portion, I decided to add letters I had written during those years, to explain as best I could what I believed, so that the reader would know not just the events but my beliefs as well.

While I was concentrating on my biography I was also composing articles of general interest relative to our country. Some were published as editorials in the Arizona Daily Star. I decided to collect them and put them in my second book. I entitled it "The Last Angry Man" because most are very negative as I railed at the lack of leadership from the major parties. These were written between 2003 and 2006. As discouraged as I was, I believed I would just stop there but I didn't? I continued to write and published my third book. It was entitled "Still Angry". It contained articles from 2006 to 2010. It began during the final years of President Bush's Administration. It ends at the start of President Obama's second year in office. And now you can continue with me analyzing the continuing ineptitude of our government leaders. I rail against them all, both parties. This latest book continues my journey of discovery starting in 2010 and continuing into 2013.

There is one thing you should know, that is that my writings are not politically correct. I do my best to say it as clearly as I can.

Read, analyze, discuss and do something for your country.

Preface

I voted for Obama in 2004. I believed the words he spoke. After the disastrous policies of Bush I think I would have voted for anyone. I did not vote for him in 2008 as I found that the things he had stated four years earlier were not the programs he actually enacted. He was re-elected to a second term. I am convinced that the American people have forgotten those stirring words "Ask not what your country can do for you, ask what you can do for your country". The Republicans don't give us a viable alternative, their only goal is to see that Obama fails.

I am still angry at the photo of President Obama nearly bent over in deference to the Royal highness of Saudi Arabia. How humiliating to see America humbled this way.

In assembling my articles and letters for the two angry man books I decided to place them in chronological order as they had been written. Reviewers were critical of this so in this book I have tried something different. Most are still in order but there are also two chapters consisting of like content. The first is entitled Biographies of Presidents other historical people and events. These were all book reports. The second is entitled Islam book reports. I decided this might make better sense than scattered throughout the book. You will note I have clearly identified radical adherents to Islam as the major threat to orderly civilization as we have known it.

My interest in Presidents was sparked by Ron Rude who taught a course in OLLI on endings of our Presidents terms. I realized how inadequate my knowledge was of Presidents before and after Lincoln. After reading my reports I would encourage you to read the books for yourself. Our history is fascinating to review. Most are available at the Public Library. By the way OLLI refers to Osher Lifelong Learning Institute. It is under the auspices of the University of Arizona and provides learning experiences for those over the age of 50. I highly recommend joining.

I allowed myself to intersperse among the serious articles things of a personal matter.

The articles and letters in this booklet were all written in the hope that someone in a position to do something might read and then put these thoughts into positive action. I do not realistically think this will happen. Perhaps all it will be is part of a legacy of this generation and may be of historical significance.

Presidents

Biographies of Presidents,
other historical persons and events

Americans today for the most part are ignorant of our history. I include myself in that condemnation. Over the past decade I have tried to rectify by reading as many books as I could to re-educate myself. The book reviews are meant to whet your appetite to read history yourself or at the very least provide you with a summary of our past. The turbulent growth is fascinating to discover. It was never easy. If you think campaigning is rough today you should read about Jefferson vs. Adams.

Some wise person coined a phrase "If you are ignorant of history you are bound to repeat the failures". I may not have quoted it verbatim but you get the idea.

Presidents;

American Lion—Andrew Jackson in the White House by; Jon Meacham
Daniel Webster's speech in defense of preserving the Union Jan 27, 1830
Excerpts from President Jackson's Second Inaugural Address
A Country of Vast Designs-James K. Polk by; Robert W. Merry
Abraham Lincoln-A man of Faith and Courage by; Joe Wheeler
Lincoln—President Elect by; Harold Holzer
Team of Rivals—The Political Genius of Lincoln by Doris Kearns Goodwin
Destiny of the Republic—James Garfield by; Candice Millard
The Forgotten Conservative-Grover Cleveland by; John M. Pafford
The Rise of Theodore Roosevelt by Edmund Morris
Theodore Rex by; Edmund Morris
River of Doubt—Theodore Roosevelt by; Candice Millard
Colonel Roosevelt by; Edmund Morris
Freedom from Fear—the American people in Depression and War, 1929-1945
    by; David M. Kennedy
New Deal or Raw Deal—F.D. R. by; Burton Folsom Jr.
Franklin and Winston by; Jon Meacham
Eisenhower—Soldier and President by; Stephen E. Ambrose

Jack Kennedy by; Chris Mathews
President Nixon deserves credit
God and Ronald Reagan by; Paul Kengor
Family of Secrets—the Bush family—by; Russ Baker

Other persons;

Patton—Ordeal and Triumph by; Ladislas Farago
This is Herman Cain—My Journey to the White House by; Herman Cain
Never Surrender—William Boykin by; William Boykin and Lynn Vincent

Historical Events;

In Black and White—Setting the Record Straight-American History by; David
  Barton
Flyboys-WWII in the Pacific by; James Bradley
Freedom's Forge—How American business produced victory in WWII by
  Arthur Herman
Unbroken by; Laura Hillenbrand
Lost in Shangri-La by; Mitchell Zuckoff
The Candy Bombers—The untold story of the Berlin Airlift and America's
  Finest Hour by; Andrei Cherny
The Help—A novel by; Kathryn Stockett
Uncle Tom's Cabin-A novel by; Harriet Beecher Stowe
Death Clouds on Mt. Baldy by; Cathy Hubault

American Lion
Andrew Jackson in the White House
By; Jon Meacham

A friend loaned me this book while I was attending Ron Rude's class on Presidential Endings. He is allowing me to make a short presentation on 2/28, 2013 to the class.

This book is very well written. It is a New York Times Best Seller published in 2009. I judge the veracity also by the number of pages of reference. This book has 100 pages.

Andrew Jackson

He was the first President from a State not one of the original 13 colonies. He was considered a man of the people not the establishment or the elite class.

He was born in March 1767 and was eight when Congress declared independence. In 1779 his older brother died while fighting the British in the Carolina's. He was living in Waxhaw, a village near Charleston which was attacked brutally by the British in April, 1781. Hundreds were killed. He was 14 when captured. An officer told him to polish his boots. He refused and was struck on his upraised hand and forehead by a sword. He carried those scars for life. It was said that he was strengthened by the blows, for he would spend the rest of his life standing up to enemies, enduring pain and holding fast until, after much trial, victory came.

His mother was a strong independent woman who cared for her two sons after the death of his father. It is said that it was from her that he obtained the fortitude which enabled him to triumph with so much success over the obstacles which have diversified his life. She was deeply religious and hoped that Andrew would become a minister. He attended Presbyterian Church services his first 14 years. Throughout life he would quote bible verses. He was most inspired by the struggle David had against Goliath and being a ruler who rose from obscurity to secure his nation and protect his people. He felt this was his destiny as well. He read the Bible daily. In the end Jackson chose to serve God and country not in a church but on battlefields and at the highest levels.

He had little formal education but was a well-read person. He did study in Salisbury N. Carolina and received his license to practice law. He worked hard and played hard. A contemporary said "He was the most roaring, rollicking, game-cocking, card-playing, mischievous fellow who ever lived in Salisbury". I added this in the interest of showing he was not a saint but had human failings as we all do.

When he was 21 he moved to Nashville, Tennessee. It was not yet a State.

He took up residence at Colonel Donelson's home who had a daughter named Rachel. She is described as a beautiful young woman with a strong sense of fun. She was married. The marriage was not a happy one. She was living in Kentucky with her husband. He was abusive so her brothers went there to bring her home. That is when she met Jackson.

In the winter of 1790-91 Jackson learned that her husband had obtained a divorce. He promptly married her. It was two years later that he found out that the husband had only filed for divorce. It was granted in 1793. They became legally married a few months later. They formed a strong bond, each giving to the other the support needed. This became a bitter subject 30 years later when running for the Presidency. There are many pages describing the close relationship they had and how much she meant to him. In 1803 in Knoxville she was insulted by Governor Sevier. Shots were exchanged between the two men. No one was hit but in 1806 another slur by Charles Dickinson led to a duel. Jackson let him shoot first. He was hit in the chest, and then he fired and killed Dickinson. He carried the bullet in his body his whole life.

As an Indian fighter it was written "Jackson's gallantry and enterprise were always conspicuous, attracted the confidence of the whites and inspired honor and respect among the savages". By projecting personal strength, Jackson created an aura of power, and it was this aura, perhaps more than any particular gift of insight, judgment, or rhetoric, that propelled him throughout his life. Once as a Judge he confronted an armed man Russell Bean. The Sheriff was afraid to bring him in but he surrendered to Jackson.

He became Attorney General of Tennessee, was elected to the U.S. House of Representatives, then the U.S. Senate, a Judge and in 1802 became a Major General of the State militia. He was 45 when the War of 1812 started. He deeply cared about the soldiers under his command and felt of them as family. There was a situation just before the war commenced while leading his troops towards New Orleans he was ordered to return. 150 were sick. He refused to leave them behind, ordering all able bodied men including him and officers to give up their places in the wagons or on horseback to the sick. It was at this time the phrase "Old Hickory" was coined.

On September 4, 1813 he confronted a man he had a disagreement with. His name was Jesse Benton. He pointed his gun but Benton shot first and hit Jackson in the upper arm. The doctor wanted to amputate but Jackson said no. A month later the Creek Indians massacred settlers in Fort Mims forty miles North of Mobile. 250 whites were killed. Even though still recovering from his wound he led forces and won a bloody victory at Tallushatchee, a Creek village. A small Indian boy was found after the battle. He adopted the boy and sent him to Hermitage to live with his family and be a playmate for his other adopted son Andrew Jackson Jr.

The Donelson family became part of the household of Jackson. When he was elected as President they lived with him at the White House. He enjoyed family and children.

He followed the Indians to Spanish Florida to drive them out of the country. Then he turned his attention to New Orleans. Dec, 16, 1814 he imposed martial law on the city, defying a writ of habeas corpus and jailing the Federal judge who issued it. He engaged the British on January 8, 1815 winning a great victory. The British lost 300 dead, 1,200 wounded and hundreds more taken prisoner. Only 13 Americans died with 39 suffering wounds. This victory elevated him to national status.

Between 1816 and 1820 he continued his battles with the Indians in the South and West, signing treaties that added tens of millions of acres to the United States. President Monroe authorized Jackson to quell the Seminole threat emanating from Spanish Florida. With that authority he did move against the Seminoles and Spanish and conquered Florida.

In 1824 he ran for President. In a four man race he garnered the most votes but not enough. The House of Representatives chose John Quincy Adams mainly due to Henry Clay who felt Jackson was not qualified to serve. Jackson was quite bitter and felt the establishment was stacked against him. Clay became Secretary of State under Adams.

His dear wife Rachel died before he was elected President in 1828. He blamed her death of the accusations of adultery from their non-marriage years ago. He won handily winning 56% of the popular vote and the Electoral College by a margin of 178 to 83. This time it was Adams who was bitter. He left Washington without attending the inauguration. John C. Calhoun was his Vice President. He gave nothing but trouble. He was from S. Carolina and was in favor of nullification. Their main complaint was the tariff which they believed favored the Northern States. The issue of secession would continue throughout both of Jackson's terms. He fought against it. He believed strongly that the Union must be preserved.

The Donelson family moved in. Niece Emily became the hostess and did well. The family was of great benefit to Jackson as a counter to the duties of being President. There are many pages devoted to them. Due to the disapproval of Emily and others to the wife of his Secretary of War John Henry Eaton, disharmony was the result. Her name was Margaret. They felt that she was not acceptable. There were unproven rumors of sexual exploits. This became intolerable to Jackson and the wives and children were returned to Nashville. This created a hardship for Jackson.

An interesting but little known piece of Legislation was proposed on December 29, 1829 by Connecticut Senator Samuel Foot. It would limit the sale of public lands in the Western part of the country, thus checking expansion and settlement. The impetus was to retain cheap labor for the manufacturers in New England. The debate continued until May 21, 1830. 65 Senators spoke. It brought forth passions on all sides including slavery and threatened to break the Union apart. Daniel Webster delivered an address that became one of the noblest passages in American canon. He strove to assure the continuation of the Union. I have handouts of this speech to share. Jackson was greatly relieved.

Jackson was the first to rely on the veto to control the Congress. The first six presidents vetoed a total of nine bills. Jackson vetoed a dozen.

He believed that America East of the Mississippi belonged to people of the white race and was determined to remove Indians from the South. The legislation was entitled "The Bill for an Exchange of Lands with the Indians Residing in Any of the States or Territories, and for Their Removal West of the Mississippi". After impassioned debate it was approved. Jackson considered himself to be a father to the Indians and was doing the right thing. He met with the Chiefs personally. He said "Friends and Brothers; You have long dwelt on the soil you occupy, and in early times before the white man kindled his fires too near to yours . . . . You were a happy people, ", Now your white brothers are around you . . . . Your great father . . . . asks if you are prepared and ready to submit to the laws of Mississippi, and make a surrender of your ancient laws . . . . you must submit-there is no alternative . . . . Old men! Lead your children to a land of promise and of peace before the Great Spirit shall call you to die. Young Chiefs! Preserve your people and nation." And so the process referred to later as the Trail of Tears began.

He was totally opposed to the Bank. Mr. Biddle, the head of the Bank encouraged Congress to extend the Charter before the election in November 1832. It did pass. In July Jackson vetoed it. The veto stood. He was vehement that the Bank was being used to influence Congress with loans and was being used as an instrument to maintain the status of the elite in the country rather than the people. Biddle's strategy backfired as the people strongly supported their president. Another accomplishment was obtaining moderate tariff reform. He hoped it would be sufficient to curtail S. Carolina's nullification efforts. In this he failed.

Jackson won re-election overwhelmingly. He carried the Electoral College by 219-49 and the popular vote with 55%. It would have been greater but a new party entered the race called Anti-Mason which believed the Mason's represented a conspiracy. (That remains to present day). Seven days later in Columbia, the South Carolina convention nullified the Tariff of 1832. What this meant was they were defying the authority of the Federal Government. Jackson took the first step to remove officers and men from Federal Forts there and replace with those who would defend the Union. There was a confrontation which could have started a conflict. I never realized that secession was so possible 30 years earlier than the Civil War. Some feared he would take action. He was determined to only strike back if attacked. In S. Carolina militias were formed, armed and trained. He gave impassioned speeches in defense of the Union and tried to lower tension by proposing legislation to incrementally lower the tariff over a ten year period but at the same time ask Congress for authority to put down rebellion with force. He got approval for both. The other Southern States decided not to support S. Carolina and in March 1833 South Carolina rescinded their previous edict and the crisis was over. However Jackson and others understood peace was only temporary and that the slave issue was still simmering and could explode at any time.

Jackson's Second Inaugural address was stated to be one of the great passages of oratory of his long public life. I have a handout of the most important parts of that speech for you.

On a steamboat trip May 8, 1833 a disturbed naval officer leaped at the president as if to assault him. Jackson was injured but the assailant was subdued. Just after this episode the president named a postmaster from New Salem, Illinois, a twenty-four year old lawyer who had lost a race for the state legislature. His name was Abraham Lincoln.

With this crisis over he concentrated on eliminating the Federal Bank. He was nearly alone. Most of his Cabinet and Congress disagreed. He took the direct approach of ordering the Secretary of the Treasury to transfer funds to state banks. He refused. Jackson fired him. The funds were transferred. The next part was confusing to me. The President of the Bank Biddle stopped lending funds to business and industry causing havoc. If the funds were no longer there how could he do that? Perhaps one of you knows. At any rate petitioners called on the President. He referred them back to Biddle. In the end Jackson won. On April 4, 1834 the House voted to not re-charter the bank. The House was elected by the people, the Senate by State legislators.

In retaliation the Senate on a 26 to 20 vote censored Jackson. It stated "Resolved, That the President, in the late Executive proceedings in relation to the public revenue, has assumed upon himself authority and power not conferred by the Constitution and Laws, but in degradation of both."

This was a severe blow followed shortly thereafter by the French government voting to not repay funds owed for damage to American ships during the Napoleonic wars violating the signed treaty. The action of France triggered tensions between the countries. Legislation was passed increasing the naval fleet and fortifying the coastal cities. France readied their frigates to attack American ships. England acting as intermediary was able to achieve a compromise. France agreed to pay the debt.

January 8, 1835 it was announced that the National Debt had been eliminated. This had been Jackson's goal from the beginning. Keeping the tariffs high had been necessary to accomplish.

Twenty two days later while walking out of the House chamber an unemployed house painter within ten feet of Jackson aimed a pistol at him. He fired. The cap exploded but it misfired. Jackson charged him with his cane. A second pistol was fired with the same result. Jackson pursued him until satisfied he was controlled.

The Seminoles refused to leave Florida. The Seminole War lasted for seven years. Americans had been settling in Mexico's Texas for some time and wanted independence from Mexico. On March 6, 1836 Santa Anna attacked and killed all the defenders of the Alamo. A month later under General Sam Huston the Mexican army was defeated. Santa Anna was taken prisoner. Jackson while happy with the outcome did not interfere as we had a treaty with Mexico.

He supported Van Buren for president through supporters. It was unseemly in those days for a president to actively engage in politics. Van Buren was elected.

Jackson's last request of the Senate was to expunge the Censor against him. After lengthy debate it was granted. With that he retired to Tennessee.

He communicated with officials with his thoughts until his death. He died peacefully surrounded by family June 8, 1845. He had lived 78 years which was remarkable in those days. On January 8, 1853 thousands gathered for the commemoration of a statue of Jackson. Senator Stephen Douglas was the keynote speaker. He pointed out that Jackson had lost his mother, father and two brothers and that orphaned he found his family in his country.

Many presidents have given praise to him. Lincoln read his Proclamation to the people of S. Carolina as he was drafting his own inaugural address. He looked to Jackson to arm himself against disunion and despair. Theodore Roosevelt said "Jackson had many faults, but he was devoted to the Union, and he had no thought of fear when it came to defending his country." FDR on a visit to the Hermitage insisted on walking with his heavy braces in respect for Jackson. In 1941 he said" Responsibility wore heavy on the shoulders of Andrew Jackson. In his day the threat was from within . . . Ours comes from a great part of the world that surrounds us . . . . "Harry Truman, while a judge in Kansas, commissioned a statue of Old Hickory to sit outside the court house in Kansas City. President Truman said "He wanted sincerely to look after the little fellow who had no pull and that's what a president is supposed to do".

Jack B. Walters
February 24, 2013

Daniel Webster's speech in defense of preserving the Union
January 27, 1830.

I have not allowed myself, sir, to look beyond the Union, to see what might lie hidden in the dark recess behind. I have not coolly weighed the chances of preserving liberty, when the bonds that unite us together shall be broken asunder. I have not accustomed myself to hang over the precipice of disunion, to see whether, with my short sight, I can fathom the depth of the abyss below; nor could I regard him as a safe councilor in the affairs of his Government, whose thoughts should be mainly bent on considering, not how the Union should be best preserved, but how tolerable might be the condition of the People when it shall be broken up and destroyed. While the Union lasts, we have high, exciting prospects spread out before us and our children. Beyond that I seek not to penetrate the veil. God grant that in my day, at least, that curtain may not rise. God grant that on my vision never may be opened what lies behind. When my eyes shall be turned to behold, for the last time, the sun in Heaven, may I not see him shining on the broken and dishonored fragments of a once glorious Union; on States dissevered, discordant, belligerent; on a land rent with civil feuds, or drenched, it may be, in fraternal blood! Let their last feeble and lingering glance, rather behold the glorious Ensign of the Republic, now known and honored throughout the earth, still full high advanced, its arms and trophies streaming in their original luster, not a stripe erased or polluted, not a single star obscured-bearing for its motto, no such miserable interrogatory as, What is all this worth? Nor those other words of delusion and folly, Liberty first, and Union afterwards—but everywhere, spread all over in characters of living light, blazing on all its ample folds, as they float over the sea and over the land, and in every wind under the whole Heavens, that other sentiment, dear to every true American heart—Liberty and Union, now and forever, one and inseparable!

Jack B. Walters
February 24, 2013

Excerpts from President Jackson's Second Inaugural Address

. . . . Without Union our independence and liberty would never have been achieved; without Union they can never be maintained, Divided into twenty-four or even a smaller number, of separate communities, we shall see our internal trade burdened with numerous restraints and exactions; communication between distant points and sections obstructed or cut off; our sons made soldiers to deluge with blood the fields they now till in peace; the mass of our people borne down and impoverished by taxes to support armies and navies, and military leaders at the head of their victorious legions becoming our lawgivers and judges. The loss of liberty, of all good government, of peace, plenty, and happiness, must inevitably follow a dissolution of the Union. In supporting it, therefore, we support all that is dear to the freeman and the philanthropist.

The time at which I stand before you is full of interest. The eyes of all nations are fixed on our Republic. The event of the existing crisis will be decisive in the opinion of mankind of the practicability of our federal form of government. Great is the stake placed in our hands. Great is the responsibility which must rest upon the people of the United States. Let us realize the importance of the attitude in which we stand before the world. Let us exercise forbearance and firmness. Let us extricate our country from the dangers which surround it and learn wisdom from the lessons they inculcate.

. . . . foster with our brethren in all parts of the country a spirit of liberal concession and compromise, and, by reconciling our fellow citizens to those partial sacrifices which they must unavoidably make for the preservation of a greater good, to recommend our invaluable government and Union to the confidence and affections of the American people.

Jack B. Walters
February 24, 2013

A Country of Vast Designs
(James K. Polk, the Mexican War and the Conquest of the American Continent)
By; Robert W. Merry

A short while ago I read a biography of Andrew Jackson. I became intrigued by the events that occurred during these years. In particular the additional territory added to the Union. While still a General during the presidency of James Monroe he conquered Florida whereby Spain ceded it to America and also added tens of millions of acres to the Union from Indian tribes in the South and West.

James Polk was supported by Jackson with advice and consul until his death. Polk became President by default. At the time he was running for Vice President. The delegates at the Democratic Convention were deadlocked. He was stunned to learn of his nomination.

Once he became President he resolved to accomplish his most important goals during one four year term and he did. The most important, in my opinion, was acquiring all remaining lands in the West including the Texas, New Mexico and Oregon territories. He added over five hundred thousand square miles and gave the United States free access to the Pacific. The total amount far exceeds the Louisiana Purchase. It encompassed all lands between America at that time and the Pacific Coast, except for a small area of 30,000 square miles in Southern Arizona and New Mexico, referred to as the Gadsden Purchase which was acquired in 1854.

This goal was popular with the people who foresaw increased opportunity as lands became available, but the job was not easy. In the Northwest England claimed ownership. There was a possibility of war between the two countries. When we relented on ceding the lower half of Prince Edward Island to Canada which gave them free access to the port at Vancouver agreement was reached. While this was going on, Polk aggressively prodded Mexico by moving troops to the Rio Grande River. Mexico responded by attacking and killing a number of soldiers. Military actions were forthcoming in Texas, New Mexico and California. Mexican ports were blockaded and Mexico City was occupied. Finally a treaty was signed ceding these lands to America.

During all this time Polk was berated for the Mexican War by politicians of the Whig Party including Daniel Webster and even a freshman Congressman named Abraham Lincoln.

Most of the problems in ending the war with Mexico had nothing to do with that country. It was the issue of slavery in the new territories. It became inescapable in August 1846. Polk was asking the Congress for $2 million to offer to Mexico, an amount he had good reason to believe would accomplish that objective.

Unexpectedly a relative unknown Congressman, David Wilmot offered an amendment forever known as "The Wilmot Resolution". It provided;

"That, as an express and fundamental condition to the acquisition of any territory from the Republic of Mexico by the United States, by virtue of any treaty which may be negotiated between them, and to the use by the Executive of the moneys herein appropriated, neither slavery nor involuntary servitude shall ever exist in any part of said territory, except for crime, wherein the party shall first be duly convicted."

This, in effect was challenging the slave states to give up on their bringing slaves to these new lands. Once again, as it was in Jackson's term the specter of cessation was breathed new life. Not only did Polk not get the money requested but the war became secondary to the issue of slavery. You can only imagine the pressure this would add during wartime.

He was under great strain during the rest of his term. While he did accomplish his goal it drastically affected his health. After his term ended he only lived four extra months dying at the age of fifty three.

I am willing to grant that he was a patriot who gave his life for his country. That is the same status I give to FDR. The strain of office also took his life. I see that as the same as dying on the field of battle. Historians in 1962 rated Polk as being in the top eight presidents at that time. After reading this biography I must concur. The greatest of leaders throughout history were the ones who pursued their objectives through thick and thin without regard to their own wellbeing. He was certainly one of those.

This is a well-researched and written book worthy of reading. It is 500 pages with a great deal of information which I have not included in this short report.

Jack B. Walters
April 23, 2013

Abraham Lincoln
A man of
Faith and Courage
By Joe Wheeler

I don't know about you but I can never get enough reading about the life of Abraham Lincoln. This particular book is very positive in all respects. It emphasizes his deep religious beliefs and the gentleness of his character. Appendix Two and Three are stories of kindness and concern in separate instances involving children. In addition, throughout the book, there are many references to his honesty and compassion. There can be little doubt that he deserves to be recognized as the greatest of all our presidents.

He learned to hate the slavery of blacks early in his life by witnessing the cruelty of those in power over the slaves. He vowed to do whatever he could to remove this curse from America. He alone deserves the recognition that it was accomplished. During the critical debates with Stephen Douglas he made this the central theme of his campaign. When he was announced as the President-elect the Southern States seceded from the Union. Prior to his taking office Washington was nearly taken over. In fact on his way to Washington there were attempts made on his life.

The early days were fraught with impending disaster. There were many instances where he could have perished but he lived on to see his dream realized, a United States of America without slavery. There has never been a man elected President from such a low estate. He thanked profusely his second mother for providing opportunities to learn to read against his father's will. His father thought learning anything other than the basics to survive was wasted effort. Thru hard physical labor Abraham developed into a very strong man. A number of times his strength was necessary for survival.

The overriding theme of this book is the strong faith that he relied on during the darkest days. He did not hide it. Many of his speeches and writings included references to God and his purpose for mankind.

In today's world our leader has asserted that we were never a Christian nation and has gone out of his way to prove his conviction. Where, oh where, is our Abe Lincoln when he is so desperately needed not just for America but for the world.

Jack B. Walters
August 4, 2010

You can ignore my last paragraph. I do recommend reading this book.

Lincoln
President-Elect
By Harold Holzer

I found this book at the Public Library. I am not going to recommend reading except for those who can absorb great detail. It is nearly 500 pages covering almost daily events between the times Lincoln was elected until his swearing in ceremony, November 6, 1860 to March 4, 1861. Much of it has to do with the endless petitioning for patronage jobs. The author introduces thousands of names I found difficult to keep track of.

Nearly four full months elapsed before he could take control. Had the process been shortened as it is today, perhaps the secession of the Southern States might have been avoided. The current President James Buchanan could not or would not take decisive action. One by one the States declared their independence from the Union. Before he was sworn in Jefferson Davis had already been elected as the President of the Confederacy.

Lincoln worked tirelessly perfecting his inaugural address hoping he could persuade the South to re-enter the Union, to no avail. In it he agreed to uphold their right to slavery and also pledged to enforce the return slave policy which had been enacted by the current Congress. The only point he would not accept was allowing slavery in States yet to be admitted into the Union. By this time the Congress had also outlawed bringing more slaves to America. Lincoln's theory was that if contained in the original States that over time it would end of its own accord.

I can only ponder what might have happened had they accepted his terms; might slavery still be in effect today?

Jack B. Walters
September 5, 2010

Team of Rivals
The Political Genius of Lincoln
By Doris Kearns Goodwin

This book is another interesting approach to understanding our greatest president; Abraham Lincoln. I have read many books on his life. They usually approach the subject from different vantages. This one reviews the lives of the members of Lincoln's cabinet leading to being appointed to his cabinet. Three of them were in the running for president against Lincoln. He chose them as he considered them to be the most capable men available and wanted their advice as he led our country thru its most perilous period.

It has 754 pages of reading, much of which requires concentration to keep the various people in the proper order since many names are made a part of this history book. It is an excellent work that required years of diligent research to compile. I am going to take a Lincoln break now even though I find his life and thinking of outstanding value.

It is available at the Tucson Public Library.

Jack B. Walters
October 4, 2010

Destiny of the Republic
A tale of madness, medicine and the murder of a President
By Candice Millard

I had the highest respect for Mrs. Millard after reading "The River of Doubt, so I looked forward eagerly to reading this book. I was not disappointed. The research that it must take to collect the information must be a massive undertaking. She is obviously very qualified in doing so. I, like most other Americans had little knowledge of President Garfield. His tenure as President was limited. He was shot after three months on the job, just getting his policies in order when it happened. He did linger on for a number of months but was incapacitated as to performing his duties.

The author weaves in Alexander Graham Bell and the invention of the telephone and his attempt to invent a device to locate the bullet in Garfield's chest. She also gives us the history of the assassin Charles Guiteau and the American medical community who did not believe there were germs. The premise is that had they done so Garfield would have recovered on his own, as he was a fit person, quite strong. All of the above were intertwined gradually ending with the shooting and then his painful death.

Garfield was born in a very small log cabin, the last President to start this way. His father died while he was just a boy. His mother did everything she could to see that he became educated and could improve himself. This part of the book is fascinating. I proves the old adage that you can become what you want to be if you put forth the effort.

From her account of his writings and life it assures me that he could have been a great President. In his inaugural address he spoke with passion about the legacy of the Civil War. He said, "The elevation of the negro race from slavery to the full rights of citizenship is the most important political change we have known since the adoption of the Constitution. It has liberated the master as well as the slave from a relation which wronged and enfeebled both".

How much might he have been able to accomplish had that madman not decided to make himself famous by murdering this wonderful man.

We will never know, but what we do know is that the black race suffered for many years trying for equality in the face of bigotry, that I might add continues today.

Jack B. Walters
June 6, 2013

The Forgotten Conservative
Rediscovering Grover Cleveland
By John M. Pafford

I have been on a personal voyage of filling in the lapses in my memory of the decades before and after the Civil War. I found this book at Barnes and Nobel while visiting family in Anchorage. It was interesting to learn that he was a Democrat who believed the government should not interfere with the private sector. He defended the Constitutional limits of federal power with resolve. He vetoed more bills than all the previous predecessors combined usually on the grounds that Congress had acted without a clear warrant in the Constitution.

He was the only President to serve two non-consecutive terms. He was a man of high integrity. This trait was why the voters respected him. All through his life that was his mantra. His rise to the Presidency in 1884 was extremely quick, just three years after being elected Mayor of Buffalo, N.Y.

There were no wars or crises to make him famous; he just did the job with prudence and skill. The biggest concern in those years was whether to base our currency on the gold or silver standard. Not a very interesting topic to read about.

He was a devout Christian and believed that divine law was the foundation of human law. The following is a quote describing his view. "It is right that every man should enjoy the result of his labor to the fullest extent consistent with his membership in civilized community. It is right that our government should but be the instrument of the people's will, and that its cost should be limited within the lines of strict economy. It is right that the influence of the government should be known in every humble home as the guardian of frugal comfort and content, and a defense against unjust exactions, and the unearned tribute persistently covered by the selfish and designing. It is right that efficiency and honesty in public service should not be sacrificed to partisan greed; and it is right that the suffrage of our people should be pure and free".

Compare his philosophy to our current leaders. I rest my case.

This not an exciting book but pertinent in comparison to where we are today.

Jack B. Walters
June 7, 2013

The Rise of Theodore Roosevelt
By Edmund Morris

This is a very well researched written account of Theodore Roosevelt's life from inception to becoming President after the assassination of President McKinley. Mr. Morris also wrote Theodore Rex which covers his years as President and Colonel Roosevelt which covers the years after. I have read Colonel and look forward to Rex.

His father was a respected and successful businessman and politician. He pushed for enactment of a bill for the appointment of unpaid Allotment Commissioners, who would visit all military camps to persuade soldiers to set aside pay deductions for family support. He was appointed by President Lincoln to carry out this job. He spent many days in the field and was successful.

As a young boy our Theodore was sickly to the point of concern whether he might die. This continued into his teen years. His wealthy father was able to take him and the family several times to visit Europe to learn and recuperate. Teddy was a good reader and student. He did all he could to increase his physical abilities. As he grew older the change was dramatic.

I can't begin to provide an interesting summary of his life other than to say he was honest, conscientious and fearless. He never backed down regardless of risk whether facing a charging grizzly bear or himself charging up San Juan Hill leading his rough riders to victory over the Spaniards in Cuba. As the Police Commissioner of New York City he brought order to the group and eliminated corruption. Earlier as a freshman N.Y. State legislature he was able to enact reform type bills. He discovered the Black Hills of N. Dakota and became a rancher. There are numerous episodes of him pursuing outlaws or fighting gun men as well as surviving intense heat and cold.

This is an 800 page biography worthy of reading. I found it at the Wilmot Public Library. I encourage you to read about one of our greatest Presidents.

Jack B. Walters
July 2, 2013

Theodore Rex
By Edmund Morris

Reading this book completed my quest to learn as much as I could about this great man. This is the third book written by Mr. Morris. It covers the seven and one half years he served as President from 1901 to 1909. His first obligation after the tragic assassination of President McKinley was to calm the nation by stating he would follow McKinley's agenda to the best of his ability. On the train ride from Buffalo to Washington escorting the late President's body he saw tragic suffering of poor miners in Southern N.Y. He realized that he had an obligation to better their lives.

There was a bitter strike by coal miner's which lasted into early winter causing hardship for many without fuel to keep them warm. He interceded and was able to reach settlement which was agreed to by both sides. It was not easy and deep resentments were created by the owners. This was amplified when he brought suit against the Northern Securities Trust for being a monopoly. The Supreme Court ruled in the companies favor but opened the door for anti-trust legislation later on.

He innocently created quite a ruckus when he invited Booker T. Washington, a black man to dine with him in the White House. The Southern Whites were outraged. During these years lynching of Negros was ongoing with the goal of keeping them in their place of near servitude.

During his first term he was successful in granting favorable tariffs for the fledging people of Cuba, was able to obtain the right of way for the Panama Canal after the Panamanians revolted against Columbia. He sent warships to assist if necessary. Not a shot was fired. There was the threat of takeover by Germany of Venezuela. A debt was owed and could not be repaid on schedule. Shots were fired by Germany withdrew their forces reluctantly adhering to the Monroe Doctrine. There could have been war but was averted through his efforts.

In the spring of 1903 he took an extensive tour of the West including Yellowstone, the Grand Canyon and Yosemite. He actually camped and hiked four days here with John Muir. It was out of this experience that he strove to preserve these treasures for all time.

The Russo-Japanese War was being fought during his first term. Through his arbitrating abilities he was able to bring them together and ended the war with the signing of the Treaty of Portsmouth on September 5, 2005. For this he was awarded the Nobel Peace Prize.

He was re-elected in 2005 to a second term by huge numbers which seemingly should have made it easy to pursue his objectives but he did have to deal with the Senate. The Legislative session was very successful for him but difficult due to the Senate which at that time was still elected by State legislatures, not popular vote. He was granted authority to proclaim historic sites without resort to Congress, twin measures establishing liability for negligent—caused accidents, granted Oklahoma Statehood, brought protection for Niagara Falls, immunity for witnesses, the Railroad Rate Regulation Act, Meat Inspection, the Pure Food and Drug Act and much more.

He was convinced that to be a great world power it was necessary to have a powerful Navy. Bit by bit the Congress provided funding. By the end of his second term America was only behind England. Trouble developed in California with a large influx of Japanese laborers who were willing to work at much lower wages. (Haven't we heard this recently?). Harsh laws were passed discriminating against them resulting in recriminations from Japan. He was able to get Japan to curb the outflow and California to ease up averting an International problem. It was at this time he stated that a Pacific War with Japan was a distinct possibility. He sent the entire battleship fleet on a Pacific "friendship" tour reaching Yokohama. This seemed to have a calming effect.

He signed Executive Orders establishing many National Forests all across the country as well as bird sanctuaries. He called together Congress, State Governors and preservation people to a three day conference to convince them all of the need to act now to preserve our beautiful country before it was destroyed. All future generations owe thanks that America still has beauty unspoiled by commerce.

There can be no doubt he was a great President who was also a loving family man who cherished his wife and children.

Jack B. Walters
July 17, 2013

The River of Doubt
Theodore Roosevelt's Darkest Journey
By: Candice Millard

What a man. His whole life he was fearless. He was a strong leader who was one of the most popular presidents in the nation's history. When President McKinley was assassinated early in his first term, Roosevelt became president. He was re-elected for a second term then retired. He became disenchanted with President Taft and ran against him as a third party candidate. He called his new party Bull Moose. While campaigning in Wisconsin he was shot in the chest. His eye glass case and manuscript in his pocked slowed the bullet but it lodged five inches in his chest. He insisted on giving his speech while exclaiming "It takes more than that to kill a bull moose". He did collect more votes than Taft but by splitting the Republican vote he gave the win to Woodrow Wilson.

This book is the story of a former President of the United States who after being defeated in 1912, did what he always did after suffering a defeat of any nature by going on an adventure that would tax him physically and included a measure of danger. This trip surpassed anything previously tried. He went on an expedition to discover and chart a river that had never been traveled before. It was called "The River of Doubt". After his return many so-called experts wrote critical reports questioning his accomplishment of discovering and charting an unknown river in the Amazon jungle of South America. Further expeditions to this area substantiated his claim.

There has never been another President to place himself in such a perilous situation. When we think of how our President's today are protected by the Secret Service it is inconceivable to think of this man placing himself, his son and the other members of the group in such danger in an area unexplored and without means of communication of any kind.

The author describes in great detail the many dangers including passing through territory populated by Indian tribes who had never encountered people other than similar tribes. Why they allowed the group to pass was never understood. Years later as more groups entered the area warfare resulted with many deaths on all sides. There were fish, snakes, reptiles and insects of all kinds that they encountered. There were deaths. Roosevelt himself came very close near the end and contemplated taking his own life to save the others as they were nearly out of food and any delay could have been fatal to them all. He didn't and pushed himself to the limit of his strength to keep going.

There were many rapids and waterfalls to portage around cutting through the dense underbrush which continually delayed progress and required incredible feats of strength. Near the end they were living on less than half rations. The author provides infinite detail of the jungle so that the reader can understand the rigorous demands on the participants. Details of the trip were from the diaries of Roosevelt and his son Kermit and the log of the commander of the expedition, Candido Mariana da Silva Rondon. The river trip was preceded by an overland journey from 12/12/1913 to 2/25/1914 which was difficult in and of itself. The river trip lasted two months from Feb.27, 1914 to April 26, 1914 when they reached a settlement. He had lost over fifty five lbs. and had a puncture wound in a leg that festered and had to be opened and drained without any pain medication.

Having completed this book I am in awe that President Roosevelt put himself in such a dangerous situation. It is well worth reading.

Jack B. Walters
August 18, 2008

Colonel Roosevelt
By Edmund Morris

There have been many books written about the life of this remarkable man and his achievements. Not all sing his praise. I have found that most of our greatest leaders have those who find fault with them for one reason or another. It is always annoying to me. No matter what great accomplishments they did, someone always feels the need to bring them down a peg. This book was not like that. It was unique in that it concentrated on a finite period of his life from 1910 until his death in 1919 at the age of 61.

The Republican Party leaders were hoping he would run again for President in 1920 but the accumulation of trauma he had endured during his life finally took him down including being shot in the chest, malaria and leg wounds during his odyssey in the wilderness of Brazil charting an unknown river.

The book begins in the spring of 1909. He had finished his seven years as President turning the reins over to William Howard Taft. He has gone to Africa on a game hunting safari. It describes the many times his life was at risk. Afterwards he embarked on a visit to the countries in North Africa and Europe. He was greeted with the greatest respect wherever he went. While in Paris he uttered the following words which to me personified the type of man he was. He was bitter that some in academia "sneered" at anyone trying to make the real world better. He said;

"It is not the critic who counts; not the man who points out how the strong man stumbles, or where the doer of deeds could have done them better. The credit belongs to the man who is actually in the arena, whose face is marred by dust and sweat and blood; who strives valiantly; who errs, and comes short again and again, because there is no effort without error and shortcoming; but who does actually strive to do the deeds; who knows great enthusiasms, the great devotions; who spends himself in a worthy cause; who at the best knows in the end the triumph of high achievement, and who at the worst, if he fails, at least fails while daring greatly, so that his place shall never be with those cold and timid souls who know neither victory nor defeat".

In my mind that is the perfect epitaph of this great man.

He became disillusioned with President Taft and when he could not win the Republican Primary he started his own party called "Bull Moose". He won more votes than Taft but with the party split Woodrow Wilson the Democrat candidate became President in 1912. Roosevelt was a progressive and I believe was more Democrat than Republican as he railed against the excessive influence on Congress by the huge Corporations. He was also the strongest and most productive of all Presidents in the preservation of wilderness areas he felt should be preserved for future generations. He believed in graduated income and inheritance taxes on big fortunes, a judiciary accountable to changing social and economic conditions, comprehensive workman's compensation acts, national laws to regulate the labor of children and women, higher safety and sanitary standards in the workplace, and public scrutiny of all political campaign spending, both before and after elections. He supported women's right to vote. He tried to establish an understanding that science and religion could co-exist without harming each other. During his years as President he appointed men of color to key positions, most of who were quickly removed under Taft. Wilson's Administration was also lily white.

At the end of another great speech he said "We, here in America, hold in our hands the hope of the world, the fate of the coming years, and shame and disgrace will be ours if in our eyes the light of high resolve is dimmed, if we trail in the dust the golden hopes of men".

As the war in Europe struggled on with losses on all sides in the millions and German U-Boats sinking scores of American vessels, he became angry with his perception of Wilson as weak and indecisive. He spoke out for increased preparedness. The country gradually shifted from isolation to participation. It is clear that without the introduction of Americans the war would have stalemated for many years longer.

Roosevelt was a prolific author of books and articles. He had great knowledge of a number of subjects which to me was extraordinary.

I can recommend reading this book by anyone interested in American history.

Jack B. Walters
August 28, 2011

Freedom from Fear
The American people in Depression and War, 1929-1945
By David M. Kennedy

My friend Jim Terlep lent me this book to read as he knows my interest in history, particularly American history, 858 pages later I have finally completed reading. It is an outstanding effort. It is the most complete and thorough report of the circumstances and the people involved during those critical decades. It is so monumental that trying to report on any one aspect would not do justice to the author.

There have been many books written about FDR, some favorable and some negative. This author tried to expose the events and in particular the New Deal Legislation enacted as to whether positive or negative. Chapter 12 puts it all in perspective as to whether it was positive or not. In my opinion it was. People's bank deposits were protected where before they had lost everything when the banks fell. The Glass-Steagall Banking act separated investing from commercial banks. (President Clinton allowed this to be repealed which started the banks on their reckless behavior with devastating consequences. To this date our current President and Congress have not seen fit to re-enact.). Social Security was created to provide funds necessary to help the elders to live decent lives. Unions were allowed to grow to provide security and improve the lot of workers. Child labor was abolished. Many roads, bridges, dams, hiking trails, clinics, and schools were built by Americans working for the CCC or WPA.

In all the history of America up until then the Federal Government was not a factor in the economy of the country. The States had the most power but even there the free market system had nearly total control. There were many factors at play which resulted in the Depression, mostly from overproduction of farms, the dust bowl and irresponsible speculation in the markets. Over half of America lived of small farms. When the prices for agriculture products fell the suffering began. President Hoover attempted to stabilize market prices with limited success. It was FDR's New Deal that really got the Federal Government into the process of correcting imbalances when the market place proved inadequate to the challenge. Were there programs that failed, yes, but then again there were programs that worked. Most important of all was the positive effect of FDR's communication with the people. In spite of their hardship they believed their President was doing all he possibly could to relieve their suffering.

Columnist Dorothy Thompson summed up FDR's achievements in 1940 with these words, "We have behind us eight terrible years of a crisis we have shared with all countries. Here we are, and our basic institutions are still intact, our people are relatively prosperous and most important of all, our society is relatively affectionate. No rift has been made an unbridgeable schism between us. The working classes are not clamoring for communism. No country is so well off".

The author takes us step by step in the buildup to WWII. He is convinced that the Versailles Treaty written after WWI planted the seeds that resulted in the Second World War. In it Germany was made to accept full responsibility for the conflict and onerous reparations demanded to compensate the Allies for their costs. This created great hardship for the German people and created an atmosphere where a radical like Adolf Hitler could come to power. He brought them out of their Depression by ignoring the treaty and beginning his military buildup. The comment is made that had we rearmed as they did we could have risen out of the Depression faster than we did. Certainly the results of building the "Arsenal of Democracy", the Depression was over.

There is a chapter on the buildup and the genius of American Industry leaders to switch overnight from peacetime manufacturing to military. Henry Ford and Henry Kaiser were in that group. Ford created a factory from the ground up to produce B-24s. He produced 18,000 B-24s in four years. At its peak a B-24 rolled off the line every sixty-three minutes. Kaiser built twenty-seven hundred Liberty Ships. By 1943 a ship was launched every forty-One days. These were remarkable achievements and were representative of all of American industry. By war's end we had produced 5,777 merchant ships, 1,556 naval vessels, 299,293 aircraft, 634,569 jeeps, 88,410 tanks, 11,000 chain saws, 2,283,311 trucks, 6.5 million rifles and 40 billion bullets.

He takes us thru the war years capturing the important events including battles and leadership conferences. I will not attempt to list them. You should read for yourself. He is quite thorough.

See page 857 for his conclusion as follows;

"An astounding fact is that the United States at the end of the war commanded fully half of the entire planet's manufacturing capacity and generated more than half of the world's electricity. America owned two-thirds of the world's gold stocks and half of its monetary reserves. The United States produced two times more petroleum than the rest of the world combined;

it had the world's largest merchant fleet, a near monopoly on the emerging growth industries of aerospace and electronics, and, for a season at least, an absolute monopoly on the disquieting new technology of atomic power.

By wars end unemployment was negligible. In the ensuing quarter century the American economy would create twenty million new jobs. Within less than a generation the middle class more than doubled. By 1960 the middle class included almost two-thirds of all Americans. As he concludes, small wonder that Americans chose to think of it as the good war. It was a war that had brought them as far as imagination could reach, and beyond, from the ordeal of the Great Depression and had opened apparently infinite vistas to the future".

Jack B. Walters
June 3, 2011

New Deal or Raw Deal
By; Burton Folsom, Jr.

The author is a professor of history at Hillsdale College. He is a highly respected historian. I was given a copy of this book and another entitled "The New Deal" which includes thoughts of eight authors including Professor Folsom.

The occasion was a visit to Tucson by Mrs. Ellen Donovan, the Executive Director of the Founders Campaign. I have been receiving the monthly copies of Hillsdale's publication Imprimus since the mid 70's. I was recovering from pneumonia at the time and a friend gave me a copy to read and enrolled my name on the mailing list. I enjoyed reading it and the hundreds of copies since. I was also invited to attend a two day seminar last year in Tucson. I admire the college's commitment to excellence and in particular adhering to the principles as outlined in our Constitution and Bill of Rights. All students are required to take a course with this as the subject. To maintain integrity the college refuses all funds from the Federal Government. It is able to do so thru the contributions of like minded supporters. During our breakfast session I enjoyed our conversation. It was a good give and take. I was able to present my ideas and in fact gave Mrs. Donovan a copy of my latest book "Still Angry". She later wrote that she enjoyed reading. Feeling full of myself I later mailed her copies of my first two books. I also took the occasion to continue contributing financially.

Realizing that Mr. Folsom's book would be negative, I expressed that I would read them, but knew I would not enjoy it as FDR was my boyhood hero. I was 13 when Japan attacked Pearl Harbor. He was our trusted leader. We had full confidence that under his leadership that we as a nation would prevail over our enemies. The record shows that this was true. I was too young to have knowledge of the "New Deal", but remember chills would run up and down my spine as I listened to his "Fireside Chats". His charisma and enthusiasm calmed the nation and galvanized all of us to work together in our common cause. Except for the too few years of John F. Kennedy's presidency no other President has been able to create solidarity as did FDR. I even exclude President Reagan. He was a good leader but he did not create the same unity of purpose of Americans.

This book only briefly covered WWII. It was mostly about the 30's starting with President Hoover and then FDR. It chronicles many programs which were not as effective as they should have been. I will not argue with the facts as presented. The conversations reported undoubtedly took place and the failure of some of his programs did occur.

In stating my comments I want to start by suggesting that Professor Folsom is younger than I and therefore whatever information he possessed to publish this book was garnered from other sources. It is immediately evident that for whatever reason he started this project with an intense dislike of FDR. He starts by pointing out that he came from a wealthy family, was an average student or athlete. FDR's passion it seems was politics which started at an early age. The author makes the point that FDR was a liar and had a mistress and therefore unworthy of the office of President. My response is that FDR liked to use stories of made up people to drive home a point similar, if I may be so bold, as Jesus Christ did with his parables. Those were not true stories, they were meant to drive home a message. As to the mistress, I will not fill up these pages by listing the many other Presidents who transgressed in a similar vain. My position on this subject is that we are all earthly creatures with needs and wants that need to be fulfilled one way or another. In FDR's situation his marriage was for convenience, not love, at least not of a physical kind. I judge a person, not by indiscretions, but by deeds. The ultimate answer rests on whether the world was a better place because of that person's effort. In my opinion FDR certainly qualifies.

When he took office America was in a deep depression partly as a result of the extravagant policies of president Hoover. Of particular concern were the extremely high tariffs enacted the Smoot-Hawley Tariff Act. The direct result was retaliation from the other major countries. FDR campaigned against it. The author's dissatisfaction with FDR was the length of time he took to lower tariffs. He tried a country by country approach which while effective was not done as quickly as it perhaps should have been.

There is a chapter of the favorable response from the news media as if they were not doing their job of assessing him critically enough. He mentions that they did not photograph him as the cripple he was nor did they expose his love affair. FDR believed he needed to be seen as a strong leader not one crippled from polio. My reaction to this is that there were unwritten rules of conduct in those days and respect. I find that far more preferable than today when every aspect of a leader's life is exposed causing concern to citizens when they should only be concerned with leadership or lack thereof. I did not like reading that the Administration used licensing of air ways to reward or punish radio stations depending on their support or lack thereof. I was also disturbed that the various agencies such as WPA determined the disbursement of funds for political advantage. I know he wasn't the first or the last to use his position to garner political support. The author admits this but justifies his criticism that FDR had more options than previous administrations. Politics is not pretty. All thru our history parties and politicians have taken every advantage to improve their chances. Gerrymandering voting districts is one example. To this day it is par for the course. It is the voter's responsibility to understand and sort thru the rhetoric as they make their decisions.

Farm subsidies are listed as misguided. He does admit that support for agriculture started with Hoover. I think he should write a book about this subject alone and how it has continued for 70 years since FDR increasing year by year. What FDR was trying to do was spare the family farmer from the vagaries of adverse weather and market deviations. By setting support levels he hoped to aid them. My own grandfather was a successful dairy farmer who lost his farm when the banks collapsed and lived the rest of his days in poverty in a tarpaper shack. Today's subsidies go mainly to the super rich like Ted Turner who owns hundreds of thousands of acres in New Mexico. Farm families can no longer compete with the mega farms. I have written many times that aid should be restricted to the family farm but the beat goes on regardless of which party is in control. One of FDR's real successes was bringing electricity to the farms. It was not economically possible without government assistance.

I was particularly upset with his attack on Social Security. He points out that early on people who had only paid a short while received multiple windfalls. Ida Fuller paid in $24.75 and received over her lifetime $22,888.92. He is outraged. I say wonderful. This woman was given the opportunity to live out her years in dignity. When my father died he took his pension with him. My mothers' only source of income was $350/month from Social Security. My sister and I aided as best we could but both of us had three children to raise making it difficult. Before Social Security old people had nothing of their own. Could it have been better designed, probably, but regardless it fills a need even today. The fact that it is in trouble is not FDR's fault, it is every Administration and Congress since his time to make necessary corrections to keep it solvent. FDR also wanted health care for all. He didn't accomplish it. The Obama solution is an abomination in my humble opinion.

I agree with the general proposition that lower tax rates are good for the economy. It leaves funds available for individuals to spend on other than basic needs and it provides funds for industry to purchase equipment to improve their profitability. Lowering business taxes also improves the situation in regard to foreign competition. During the war FDR tried to get Congress to tax all personal income over $25,000 at 100%. The Congress balked but did set it at 90%. $25,000 was a lot of money back then. FDR did not believe it was right to profit extravagantly while 12 million men were in uniform putting their lives on the line. Contrast that with today when CEO's and other top officers of companies rake in millions every year while our boys are dying in Iraq and Afghanistan. That is what I call outrageous.

To prove his case that the New Deal was a failure he compares published unemployment statistics. The US was still at 19.8% in 1938. Guess what, Germany was at 2.1%. Looks like we would have been better off if we had started re-arming as Germany did.

FDR did not believe in relief without work except where absolutely necessary. That is why he promoted the WPA, CCC and other programs with the idea of providing useful work for those unemployed. I have hiked on trails and slept in shelters built at that time. Contrast that to today where millions have been receiving unemployment benefits of $300 or more per week to stay home. This is a continues program that is extended over and over to keep the funds flowing to people in their prime working years who could be contributing to our nation's well-being.

He didn't mention it but one of the greatest programs FDR got approved was the GI Bill of Rights. It enabled millions of veterans including myself to receive education to expand our opportunities. Together we transformed America.

In summation it comes down to this, within the framework of our Constitution, is it the responsibility of the Federal Government to take steps to correct problems or should it just sit by and let the markets run their course without stepping in to protect citizens? Just wait for the next war opportunity to do their thing. I say no. I also say that the government since Roosevelt has gone far overboard in asserting their authority such as Obama using the Commerce Clause to force citizens to purchase health insurance. It is now heading to the Supreme Court. Should they not find it un-constitutional then our great experiment in government will be over. The Dept of Energy was created in 1977 by President Carter to assure our independence in the field of energy. I understand it costs billions each year. You must know how successful that has been.

As I stated at the outset I knew I would be unhappy reading these books. It took awhile to accomplish as it was demoralizing to me. Roosevelt was my boyhood hero and even after reading these books I still feel the same. His philosophy was the same as mine during my leadership years. If there is a problem, gather together the best minds you can and brainstorm. When the best thought of solution is agreed to, assign it to staff with the knowledge and skill to enact. Should it not be the solution, then try again.

Did he make mistakes, certainly, as did I, but he kept searching for solutions? That is why the American people embraced him. He did his best. He was frustrated with the Supreme Court which kept him from enacting some of his programs which is why he foolishly tried to pack the Court. He lost a lot of support at that time. I will not condemn him for trying. Abraham Lincoln and Franklin Delano Roosevelt were our greatest presidents. John Fitzgerald Kennedy could have been the third but he was cut down before he could reach that level. All of them had personal problems but putting that aside they all strove for a better America and that is how I rate our leaders.

Jack B. Walters
March 26, 2011

Franklin and Winston
(An Intimate Portrait of an epic friendship)
By Jon Meacham

Knowing of my very high regard of FDR and Churchill, an old friend told me about this book. I have just finished reading. Over the years I have read countless books relating to WWII and the persons involved. What this book offers is a more in depth discovery of the many episodes where their lives came together during that monumental period in our history.

In the interest of keeping an open mind I have also read books by authors who do not consider them as I do. No writing by any person can result in lessening my beliefs that without these two giants the world might be an altogether different place and not for the better. Under their inspired leadership the Allied Powers defeated Nazi Germany, fascist Italy and the Empire of Japan. These were powerful adversaries prepared for conflict where we were not. Isolationism was very strong in America. FDR had to take very small steps to get us rebuilding our military strength.

The relationship grew steadily during the course of the conflict. At first when England stood alone Churchill was desperate to receive military hardware to be able to stave off defeat. Out of that came the 50 old destroyer deal followed by lend-lease. Once Russia was attacked they also received the weapons they needed.

The book also includes intimate sections relating to each of their families. The support received was very important in aiding them to enjoy family times even while under extreme pressure. Rather than try to report on any specific situation between them, all I will do is highly recommend reading this book. If you do, I'll bet you will have a better understanding and perhaps will feel as the vast majority of Americans did when FDR was elected to a fourth term as President. We could not stand to not have him leading us. My book is available to any interested person.

Jack B. Walters
May 29, 2012

Eisenhower
Soldier and President
By: Stephen E. Ambrose

Stephen Ambrose has written many historical books. I consider him one of the best. When I was informed about this new book, I immediately purchased it, even though I have read other books on the life of Dwight Eisenhower. I was not disappointed. It did advance my knowledge and understanding of the great contributions to our country and the world of this special human being. Rather than my usual assessment of a book I have chosen to just let the author speak for himself.

"His greatest successes came in foreign policy, and the related area of national defense spending. By making peace in Korea, and avoiding war thereafter for the next seven and one-half years, and by holding down, almost single-handedly, the pace of the arms race, he achieved his major accomplishments.—he rebuffed Symington and the Pentagon and the JCS and the AEC and the military-industrial complex. And no one knows how many lives he saved by ending the war in Korea and refusing to enter many others despite a half-dozen and more unanimous recommendations that he go to war."

In my opinion only Ike with his WWII record could have held back the war lovers. Any President without his credentials would have been considered soft.

He was adamant about the need to balance the budget and was successful in achieving that goal while Americans enjoyed prosperity as never before.

This is a very readable book, extremely interesting with many insights into his decision making process. His party expected him to reverse the 16 years of control by the other party but he took the best of both and formed alliances to assure the steady progress the country enjoyed. President Eisenhower is on my short list of the greatest Presidents in our history.

Jack B. Walters
April 30, 2011

53

Jack Kennedy-Elusive Hero
By; Chris Mathews

I found this book at the library. It is an in depth study of his life starting as a child and student. It is not my type of book. While filled with facts I just didn't feel the real Jack Kennedy, none the less I would recommend reading for anyone interested in his life and Presidency. He was always bold and willing to push the envelope whether in school, the Navy or politics. He was always his own man, never willing to lean too much on others.

I will confine this review to statements made by Ted Sorensen and Jackie Kennedy.

Ted Sorensen—"An American President, commander in chief of the world's greatest military power, who during his presidency did not send one combat troop division abroad or drop one bomb, who used his presidency to break down the barriers of religious and racial equality and harmony in this country and to reach out to the victims of poverty and repression, who encouraged Americans to serve their communities and to love their neighbors regardless of the color of their skin, who waged war not on smaller nations but on poverty and illiteracy and mental illness in his own country, and who restored the appeal of politics for the young and sent Peace Corps volunteers overseas to work with the poor and untrained in other countries—was in my book a moral president, regardless of his personal misconduct."

Jackie Kennedy—She gave a four hour monologue to Teddy White of Life magazine. The article was read by millions around the world. They accepted her widow's vision; they took to their hearts the notion of Camelot; that vanished, shining place presided over by a noble, merry hero.

One last thought that was brought out in this book was his aversion to sending combat troops into Vietnam even though pressured to do so by his military staff. Early in the book there were comments about France fighting to maintain their colony there, so his aversion came early in life. I am totally convinced that he would not have allowed combat troops into that country. With his death the flood gates were opened. We all know how that came out.

He did avert doomsday by keeping the military from bombing Cuba which could have resulted in Russia taking over Berlin and perhaps retaliation using nuclear weapons. We as a country and as a people were starting to regain our confidence. With his death followed shortly by King and then Bobby brought this all to an end from which we have never recovered.

Jack B. Walters
June 9, 2012

President Nixon deserves credit

He deserves credit for coming to the aid of Israel during their 1973 Yon Kipper war with Egypt and Syria. Israel was nearing the end of having sufficient military equipment to continue. General Moshe Dayan advised Prime Minister Golda Meir that they were approaching the point of last resort i.e. the nuclear option. Henry Kissinger learned of this the morning of October 9. That same day President Nixon ordered the commencement of Operation Nickel Grass, an American airlift to replace all of Israel's losses. 8,755 tons were received before the end of the war. Supplies were provided by airlift and by sea, a total of over 112,000 tons including F-4 fighters, A-4 attack airplanes, 12 C-130 Cargo planes, and every other type of equipment requested by Israel. It ended by the end of December at a total cost in today's dollars of $4.19 billion dollars.

As a sidelight to all this, only two European countries allowed our planes landing rights; Portugal and the Netherlands, so much for NATO support in time of need. Another sidelight was Henry Kissinger demanding that Israel not conduct a first strike as they had done in 1967. He said Israel would not receive "so much as a nail". I am sure Israeli losses were much greater by waiting until attacked by Egypt and Syria.

Had President Nixon not acted with such powerful full out support, it is conceivable that Israel might have been forced to use tactical nuclear weapons. What the consequences of that might be is open for conjecture. He did the right thing while in the middle of the Watergate investigation. I say give him the credit deserved.

Jack B. Walters
June 11, 2012

GOD
And
Ronald Reagan
A spiritual life
By Paul Kengor

I have a good friend at my church who reads as much or more than I do. She is a Christian in every sense of the word. Her first name is Ausma. She handed this book to me to read with the admonition that she knew I had been disillusioned by the policies of Reagan when he was president. She wanted me to understand the depth of his Christianity. This book clearly states the truth of her thinking.

It doesn't change my thinking in regards to legislation passed during his years in office. I won't take your time now by listing them. There were many that have led to the disasters we are living with today. Be that as it may, this book opened my eyes to the essential goodness of this man and his life long belief in Christianity and his resolve to help all peoples everywhere enjoy the freedom to live with their beliefs without fear of persecution as was happening so severely in the Soviet Union and the satellite states under their control.

This book takes us to his childhood with a devout mother and influential clergy who were close to him. He offended the communist elite in Hollywood by railing against that ideology. His greatest success was opening up Russia and to some extent China and allowing religious freedom. Premier Gorbachev must also be given credit. Reagan felt that deep down Gorbachev was a Christian. At any rate Reagan throughout his years in office did everything he could to accomplish this goal. It was of course successful. The Berlin wall did come tumbling down and the Soviet Union was dissolved with the satellite states regaining their rights to function as free countries.

The above was the result but reading the book gave me an insight into the deeply held beliefs he had and how they were developed and nurtured along the way. I now have a much greater understanding of this unique personality who was our president during the perilous cold war years.

I recommend reading to those who enjoy history and believe religion can be a positive influence.

Jack B. Walters
May 3, 2010

Family of Secrets
By Russ Baker

The Bush Dynasty, America's Invisible Government,
and the hidden history of the last fifty years

This is another difficult book to read. To start with it contains 494 small print pages. It includes comments about many people who were not familiar to me nor will they be to you either. Trying to keep the names in mind as you are reading is very difficult. Since the book covers fifty years of history, events a long time ago which were not generally known added to my problem? Having said all the above, the sum total of the information presented is not favorable to the Bush family. It shows an obsession with money and power. Their network of friends includes the rich and famous, many of whom were granted favors without regard to the best interest of either America or the world in general.

The author even questions the heroism of George H. W. Bush when he bailed out during the war in the Pacific. Could he have saved the lives of his two crewmen by making a sea landing? He weaves in many suggestions about culpability in the death of President Kennedy. He proves that "poppy", as he refers to the first Bush President, was in Dallas the night before the assassination and that a close friend had been an advisor to Oswald suggesting an involvement in the events leading to Kennedy's death. He devotes many pages to give food for thought about many people in Dallas at the time that were filled with hatred towards the president.

All thru the book "poppy" is shown to have been involved with the CIA, not just when he became Director but many years before. He makes his case that the first Gulf war was for oil and no other reason. Saddam had been assured that invading Kuwait would not be objectionable to America, but when he did, President Bush immediately organized a coalition of nations including Arab nations to drive Iraq out of Kuwait.

Many years before the Bush family cultivated a friendship with the Saudi rulers who provided financial support for any number of the projects of benefit to the family.

Of particular interest to me was the life of George Bush. He lived the life of privilege. A party animal, he enjoyed drinking and womanizing and is accused of getting two women pregnant both of whom had abortions. That possibility was particularly heinous to me with his ranting about "Pro Life" during his years as President. As the son of a sitting president he was given financial support for a number of efforts such a acquiring the Texas Ranger Baseball team. I never gave this man credit for smarts but the author does. George was a great salesman who could convince many to invest in risky ventures.

During his years as President he was known for giving quick responses to issues rather than exploring in depth. He was quoted as saying that a president needed a war to accomplish his agenda. He was proved right. After 9/11 and his two wars the Congress gave him whatever he requested. As President he had a total disregard to the efficient operation of government agencies by staffing them with people opposed to the mandate of those agencies. Any and all who resisted were removed. The ineffectiveness of FEMA during Katrina was a glaring example of the result of his efforts.

The author believes that G. Bush was allowed to join the Texas Air National Guard thru the influence of "poppy", ahead of many who were more qualified. This of course kept him out of Vietnam. After two years he mysteriously missed taking a mandatory physical necessary to continue flying and was taken out of flying service. He then somehow transferred to Alabama. No one seems to have ever seen him on base and his military records were conveniently lost. He was granted an honorable discharge somehow. The hypocrisy of all this was his campaign to discredit Senator Kerry's patriotism while serving in Vietnam. Somehow with the help of the "Swift Boat" campaign, Kerry's lead in the polls evaporated leading to victory for Bush.

There is much, much more. You need to read for yourself.

Jack B. Walters
January 5, 2011

Other
Persons

Patton
Ordeal and Triumph
By; Ladislas Farago

832 pages of the life of this man who became the best General officer the US Army ever had. I followed his career as a young boy but of course never had the opportunity to understand his history before the war. This book was used as the foundation for the movie PATTON starring George C. Scott. I would be ashamed to tell you how many times I have watched it. Scott did an outstanding job of re-creating this complex man. If you have seen the movie then much of this book will remind you of it. Many of the famous statements Patton made in real life were in this book and also in the movie.

Because of his impetuous nature he put himself in difficulty many times. We must credit General Marshall and General Eisenhower for recognizing how important Patton was for the war effort that they overcame the criticism and gave him command of the Third Army shortly after the Normandy landings. He was able to imbue his officers and men with his aggressive nature and went on the attack. The book mentions the numerous times when he was deliberately deprived of fuel and ammunition in favor of the British General Montgomery. The writer is convinced as am I that had he been supported fully the war could have ended in 1944. I am sure there are other books that would disagree. You can look for them. For me I am satisfied with my own point of view.

If you are a history buff as I am and in particular the Second World War then you will enjoy reading this biography.

Jack B. Walters
September 7, 2011

This is
Herman Cain
My journey to the White House
By Herman Cain

I detest the fact that political campaigning has become a forever activity but I did happen to watch a little of the second Republican debate. There on the end of the line was a man who happened to have a black complexion who was a man I had never heard of before. He was obviously not a politician. His comments intrigued me. Soon thereafter I received an e-mail listing his many accomplishments in life. I didn't believe it so I checked it out on the internet. It was true. Then a friend told me he had written a book so I checked Amazon and sure enough he had, not one book but many. Most dealt with his management philosophy. The one I purchased is the one I will be reviewing.

There are many things I like about this man. He rose out of humble beginnings in the South where blacks were discriminated against. He greatly admires his father who raised a family under these adverse conditions with dignity. The Civil Rights activity was in full swing when Herman was in High School. His father insisted he apply himself to his studies and not get involved. This he did. I heard a commentator on MSNBC deriding him for this. His father also told him to not play the victim card but do the best he could to achieve his goals. He has lived this advice.

Another thing I like is that he tells people he is an American who happens to be black. He does not use the term African/American. I have always disliked that term including other nationalities. He never uses a teleprompter. He speaks using his mind not what someone wrote out for him to say. As an aside I have heard him sing. He has a rich baritone voice. I caught the end of a speech he was giving in which he ended by singing. The audience was stunned.

He is not campaigning like all the rest. He probably will not raise much in the way of corporate contributions but with his style and speaking ability I believe he will strike a cord with those who are dissatisfied with the status quo. The fact that in such a short time he leaped to the top of the polls last week, even higher than Romney means that voters are starting to recognize who he is and what he stands for. During the debate last night, all of the other contenders beat up on him as best they could trying to knock him down before he can catch on. They all ridiculed his 9-9-9 tax plan. I don't believe they will be successful. I don't know if it is the right plan but I do know that our tax code is thousands of pages long replete with countless loopholes. I have always claimed that simplifying and closing these loopholes could result in a much lower income tax. Mr. Cain is at least brave enough to put out a plan, none of the others have. They just utter platitudes about taxes being too high without offering ideas on what to do about it.

Let me just say, you should read his book. If you do, you will be astounded, as I was, to realize his many achievements. He has turned around failing businesses and made them profitable. He is on many Boards of Directors and has received multiple awards for his success. In the book he states his ideas on how to return America to the great nation it once was and could be again. I won't state that I agree with all of his positions, but I agree with enough to be excited about what he could achieve for America. Read it and learn for yourself. You won't believe the skill this man possesses. I have no doubt he could be successful in this most important of all jobs, the Presidency of the United States of America.

Jack B. Walters
October 19, 2011

Never Surrender
A soldier's journey to the crossroads of faith and freedom
LTG (Ret.) William G. Boykin

Former commander of U.S. Army Special Forces
and founding member of Delta Force
With Lynn Vincent

I had received an e-mail which contained a speech General Boykin had made recently. It was stirring, full of his religious beliefs and the threat facing our nation from radical Muslim terrorists. Many of you receiving a copy of this book report will recognize that this has been a subject of great interest to me ever since we discovered the great hatred that exists in the radical element of persons professing to be Muslim believers.

As the General describes his life journey, I was reminded of a recent book about Ronald Reagan. Both men had extremely religious mothers who nurtured their faith at an early stage sufficient to carry them thru life.

Most of the book follows his growth thru his Army service. It was interesting to find he was a member of the first Delta Force organized for hostage rescue and quick raids to capture enemies. I received a whole new perspective on the planned raid to rescue the 54 Americans held hostage by Iranians during Jimmy Carter's presidency. The preparation on the part of Delta was thorough. The mission could have been successful except for the failure of the Navy helicopters to carry them to the Embassy in Tehran. A minimum of six were required. Only five were in good enough shape to fly, so the mission was scrubbed. One of them on takeoff crashed into a plane carrying Delta force men creating havoc. I will let you read to learn more.

He was also on the raid to capture Noriega in Panama and was the commander in Somalia where he ordered the raid to capture enemies and disaster occurred with the loss of many good men. If you have seen the movie "Black Hawk Down" you will be interested in his perspective and how deeply the loss of so many good men impacted him.

His last four years of service to his country was in the Pentagon as Deputy Undersecretary of Defense for Intelligence. It was during these last years that he started participating in giving speeches to Christian assemblies. He spoke as a devout Christian and his concern for the threat to America from radical

Islamists. The news media took after him with a vengeance. How dare he do this while wearing his uniform? After extensive investigation he was exonerated but I am sure the conflict led to his decision to retire. He still speaks out today. I am one who supports him totally. Wake up America.

Jack B. Walters
December 3, 2010

Historical
Events

Setting the Record Straight
American History
In Black & White
By David Barton

I was informed about this book and immediately ordered a copy from Amazon.com. It is only 138 pages long but is chock full of information some of which I was well aware and others that even though occurring in my life time I had forgotten or just never realized how bad it was.

Having just finished reading a book about President Lincoln and the Civil War I was cognizant of the situation during those years but the years following I had never studied until the years following WWII the Democratic Party was dedicated to keeping the black people in America in their place.

The Republican Party was created by people who were opposed to slavery. Lincoln became their first President.

Some people have claimed that the Constitution was a racist document. The author disputes that and I concur with him. The reason stated is that black men were counted as 3/5 of a person. The reason was that the Southern States wanted to count them to increase the number of representatives they would have in the Congress. The compromise reached was 3/5. It recognized the reality of slavery at the time we were breaking off the yoke of England. It was not the time to try to eliminate slavery. That would have to wait for another time. It is indisputable that the Democratic Party both North and South supported slavery. The Civil War was fought because of their insistence that slavery be extended into the new States being created in the Western part of the Continent.

Following the Civil War the Southern States were ordered to change their Constitutions prohibiting slavery. This they did. For a few years blacks voted and became legislators in these States but as time went on the Southern Democratic Party removed some of the protections afforded the blacks and began to systematically harass and did all manner of things to keep them from voting in addition to segregating education, housing, eating establishments, etc. They were kept as virtual slaves for over 80 years following the XIII and the XIV Amendments to the Constitution in 1865 and 1868. Not one Democrat voted in favor of the XIV Amendment.

In 1893 Grover Cleveland Alexander was elected President. He was a Democrat and the majority of the House and Senate were Democrats. It was then that the Congress started turning back the clock on rights and actually attempted to repeal the XIII and XIV Amendments in 1900. There were enough Republicans to prevent that from occurring. Think about what I just wrote, Democrats wanted to re-institute slavery in 1900. That is just 110 years ago.

During the decades after the Civil War blacks were controlled not only by legislatures and law enforcement but also by the KKK. The author contends the KKK was synonymous with the Democratic Party.

FDR was the first Democrat to want to do something for the blacks but had his hands full with WWII. His wife Eleanor did resign from the DAR when they refused to allow Marion Anderson to sing at their annual convention. Truman did take action. He desegregated the military. He attempted to pass civil rights legislation which caused the Southern Democrats to break away and form the Dixiecrat Party. President Eisenhower tried to pass civil rights bills and faced stiff opposition from Democrats. It wasn't until Kennedy that a Democratic President took action to integrate schools and after his death Lyndon Johnson was able to get Kennedy's Civil Rights programs enacted into law.

He doesn't explain how in recent years the black voters have turned to the Democratic Party to sustain them. Perhaps it is the never ending give away programs which while giving support at the same time create dependency whereas the Republicans want people to work and sustain themselves without government handouts. I just wonder if keeping them poor, ignorant and dependent is the new age strategy of the Democratic Party.

If you want to be better informed about our history I highly recommend reading this book.

Jack B. Walters
October 7, 2010

Flyboys
By James Bradley

Mr. Bradley also authored Flags of Our Fathers. I have read both books. He is another author that does extensive research before writing. This included personal visits with Japanese soldiers who were involved with captive flyers on the Island of Chichi Jima. This was an outpost manned by 35,000 soldiers. It had two mountain peaks which had been used to install radio equipment for communication to Japan. It was located near to Iwo Jima. There were eight prisoners. Only one lived. He had been sent to Japan and survived the war. Another pilot shot down near the island was rescued by a submarine. His name was George H.W. Bush. The two crew members in his plane did not survive.

One by one the prisoners were executed after being stabbed with sharp sticks or bayonets. They were then beheaded and in a number of instances their livers and strips of flesh from their thighs were cut out and fed to officers. This all came to light during interrogation. The details were filled in by Mr. Bradley hunting down and persuading soldiers to tell their story.

The main story is about these men as young lads who eagerly signed up to be part of the Navy's Air Arm, some as pilots, others as gunners or radio men. We get to know them and their families.

Woven into the book is a snapshot of how brutal the war was on both sides. The Japanese soldiers were treated harshly by their officers and non coms. They were taught to obey all orders without question. If they died it was for the Emperor and they would be rewarded. The slaughter of Chinese soldiers and civilians was carried out methodically and without any semblance of humanity.

One of the stories is about the B-24 Bombers taking off from an Aircraft Carrier to bomb Japan early in 1942. Psychologically it was effective both in America and Japan. We needed a lift from all the bad news. The Japanese were stunned that the war could come to their sacred lands. All of the planes crashed before reaching the Chinese Airfields due to the task force being discovered 200 miles short of the planned take off. To punish the Chinese over 200,000 were slaughtered in the area closest to Japan as they assumed the planes had used airfields in China.

We do not always come off as the good guys. The author traces our history leading to this latest conflict. I will let you discover the data when you read the book. Read it and get a refresher on how brutal war is.

Jack B. Walters
May 21, 2010

Freedom's Forge
By Arthur Herman

How American Business Produced Victory in World War II

This book reveals the previously untold story on how America was able to rapidly produce the materials needed for our Armed Forces to prevail over the AXIS nations. There have been countless books written about the war itself, but little about how we could not have prevailed if our industries with their skill at mass production had not done their job with such overwhelming success.

Americans still remembering the First World War were united in resisting fighting another war in Europe. As a result America was totally unprepared to engage the enemy until war material could be produced. In 1939 our military was ranked eighteen in the world just ahead of Holland. As the NAZI juggernaut swept thru Europe and Russia in 1939 and 40 the attitude gradually changed. Should England succumb America would have been cut off from the whole of that continent with the prospect of being attacked at a later time without Allies to fight with us.

The book recognizes the primary industrial leaders called forth by FDR to spur the creation of weapons. William Knudson, Henry Kaiser, Andrew Jackson Higgins and others. Much of the book traces their lives from humble beginnings to the giants of industry that they became. I found this very engaging. I am always searching for biographies of how great leaders come to be. My general assessment is that the greatest of these are people dedicated to improving themselves through hard work and study.

William Knudson was called to the Oval Office by FDR on May30, 1940 to head up a new agency to prepare for war. He signed on for zero pay for the duration. He told his daughter "This country has been good to me, and I want to pay it back". Under his leadership he gathered together industry leaders of small and large companies and received commitments to produce what was required. Of interest to me was that the military was so unprepared they didn't even know what they wanted. Industry took the lead and did provide.

The following are comments Knudsen made during these times. "No one can do what we can do if we all get together," he liked to boast. American's love of freedom, of individuality, of doing things differently from the other guy—these were the sources of strength, he believed, not weakness. He believed in the power of the average American worker—"Progress in the world is accomplished by average people," he would tell audiences—and the power of American business. "American ingenuity has never failed to cope with every specific problem before it, he told a national radio audience," and if we have your support and confidence, we will surely succeed." It turns out that it was he who coined the phrase "Arsenal of Democracy".

From 1940 until war end, the United States produced 141 Aircraft Carriers, eight battleships, 807 cruisers, destroyers and destroyer escorts, 203 submarines, and, thanks to Henry Kaiser and his colleagues, almost 52 million tons of merchant shipping. Also produced were 88,410 tanks, and self-propelled guns, 257,000 artillery pieces, 2.4 million trucks, 2.6 million machine guns and 41 billion rounds of ammunition. Total aircraft from 1942 to war's end was 324,750. This was an unbelievable achievement all through the genius of American industrialists and American workers.

Chapter 16 and 17 describe the creation and production of the B-29. Of interest to me was that the concept was visualized in June 1939 by Charles Lindbergh. Testing began in1942 and serious production in 1943.

I believe I learned something from reading this book which could be the answer to our declining industrial base. The key ingredient to the rapid change over was stimulus from the government. Industry on their own didn't have the reserves needed to build huge factories in open fields where nothing had been before and fill them with equipment necessary to produce the product designated. Contracts were awarded with a cost plus eight incentive. What if today our leaders would stoke the engine of manufacturing in a similar manner? We are all aware of how China builds factories, provides cheap energy and transportation to encourage our manufacturers to relocate there. It seems to me they have read this book. Too bad our leaders haven't. Instead of throwing billions to save the huge mega banks take those funds and restart production here in America. Well paid American workers would be paying taxes and start pulling us out of debt.

This is a must read book for those who care. I give it my highest recommendation. My book is available.

Jack B. Walters
August 8, 2012

UNBROKEN
By LAURA HILLENBRAND

This is an incredible true life account of an American born in 1917 and still alive as the book went to print. As a novel it would have been a thriller to read. What this man accomplished and how he survived under incredible circumstances is mind boggling. The author did voluminous research in uncovering and verifying the events.

The man's name is Louis Zamperini. He was uncontrollable as a boy, constantly in trouble. He discovered that he could be exceptional as a runner and he devoted his energy to improve. He nearly broke the four minute mile running in the same era as Glenn Cunningham who was the first to accomplish this feat. He competed in the Olympic Games in Germany in 1936. It was the 5000 meters race. His time was 14:46.8, the fastest time of any American that year. That was only good enough for eighth place but in the final lap he ran the fastest time ever recorded. Adolf Hitler was so impressed he wanted to meet Louie. Hitler said "Ah, you're the boy with the fast finish".

Once WWII began Louie enlisted and was placed in the Army Air Corp. He trained as a Bombardier in B-24's. He was sent to the Pacific Theatre. His odyssey began when his plane crashed into the ocean. Only the Pilot and one other crewman survived. They drifted for 47 days, finally being captured by the Japanese and imprisoned. Only the Pilot and Louie were alive. The story of survival on the raft would be enough but the worst was yet to come. He was sent to Japan as a war trophy after they discovered who he was. He sustained unrelenting punishment by sadistic guards. One in particular had an obsession about him and struck him regularly.

As the war was drawing to the end, the prisoners discovered that on August 22, 1945 all prisoners were to be executed. The Emperor told his people that the war was lost on August 15 and that all hostilities were to cease. That was all that saved them.

The physical and mental torment the prisoners had faced followed them as they were released. In Louis's case he became an alcoholic as his way of escaping reality. A chance meeting with a young Billy Graham in Los Angeles saved him. He remembered the vow he had made on the raft to give his life to the Lord and went on to be productive as a citizen and father.

I give this book my highest recommendation to read.

Jack B. Walters
July 2, 2011

Lost in Shangri-La
By; Mitchell Zuckoff

This is an interesting, fully documented, account of a plane crash in the mountains of New Guinea towards the end of the Pacific war of WWII.

It was a gripping personal interest account of 24 service men and women who were being rewarded for their service by taking a sight seeing plane ride to see a hidden valley that had recently been discovered. Only three survived the crash. They were all injured and had been burned. Without food or other basic items, after a few days rest, they were able to reach a clearing where they were spotted by a search plane. The rest of the story revolves around the natives they encounter, the rescuers who risked their lives and their final rescue.

The author states that this was a major news story which gripped the nation. No doubt it did but I have no recollection of the event. I found it to be very interesting and well written. I haven't spoiled it for you as what I have mentioned will be found by reading the jacket cover.

Jack B. Walters
July 21, 2011

The Candy Bombers
The Untold Story of the Berlin Airlift and America's Finest Hour
By Andrei Cherny

This is truly a beautiful story. I knew something about it from reading the life story of General Lemay who was in charge of the Air Force in Europe at the beginning. I was a young GI serving in Japan while it occurred. I guess we were preoccupied with our own sphere of concern to understand what was happening in Germany. This fine book filled in the gaps for me and I will guess would for you as well. This would be particularly true for those too young to have been around at that time. I highly recommend reading by anyone interested in history and in particular American history.

It begins with the joyous meeting of Russian and American soldiers at the Elbe River. This is where our forces were ordered by General Eisenhower to stop. He saw no good reason to lose more lives fighting for Berlin since the war was essentially won. The book reports that the Russians lost 350,000 men taking Berlin. That is a larger number than the West lost in the European war to date. That was a wise decision.

The Russians were brutal in their revenge; looting, raping and killing citizens of the city. The partition of Germany into four zones; Russian, English, French and American also included the city of Berlin. Each country shared in administering. As the years advanced from 1945 to 1948 animosity built between Russia and the Allies. Russia lowered the Iron Curtain over the countries to the west of Russia and was on a mission to make all Europe Communist States. They refused to co-operate on issues large or small. During these years hatred of Germans was shared by all parties. The hardships they were suffering were what were owed to them after the devastation they had brought to Europe.

In March 1948 President Truman asked the Congress for prompt passage of the Marshall Plan to save Europe. This was not acceptable to Premier Stalin. Berlin was located deep in the Russian Zone. It was supplied by narrow corridors for planes, trains and trucks. On April 1, 1948 all routes into the city were blocked except air. Air became the only way to supply the Allied Forces and the two and one quarter million citizens. An airlift was immediately started. No one had any faith it would be able to sustain a population that large. All of Truman's advisors recommended pulling out our troops and giving the city to Russia. Truman held firm. He said "We will not leave Berlin". The Chief of Staffs refused to send additional aircraft. They were overruled by Truman.

The Airlift was haphazard at best until General William Tunner arrived. Under his leadership it became a well-oiled machine with planes landing every three minutes night and day. One of the pilots was Hal Halvorsen. On one of his trips he wandered over to where German children were standing watching the planes coming in. He reached in his pocket and broke two pieces of gum and handed it thru the fence. He immediately got the idea of dropping candy with handkerchiefs as parachutes. He was able to communicate his intention. He told them to watch a plane that wiggled its wings. He did that and continued whenever he could get rations.

To make a long story short, let me just say that this small act of kindness mushroomed into a complete change between the citizens and our forces. They endured hardships thru that winter but held out in their resolve to be free. On May 1, 1949 the Russians opened the corridors and normalcy returned. American citizens were absorbed in the drama. It is suggested that President Truman was elected for a large part because of "Operation Candy Bombers".

I found this book at the Tucson Public Library.

Jack B. Walters
September 22, 2010

The Help
By Kathryn Stockett

This is a novel that deems to tell the story of what it might have been like to be a black woman maid for a white family. The author lived in Mississippi during the 60's which is the time period of the book. The 60's were a turbulent period as the black people, particularly in the South, started to attempt to break out of the strict class segregation that was in effect with separate schools, wash rooms, libraries, stores, etc. Martin Luther King was the leader that made it visible. He strived for peaceful resolutions as opposed to violence. President Kennedy got involved more than previous presidents. It was Lyndon Johnson who finally enacted legislation to force change.

The story is about a young white girl who dreams of becoming a writer and decides to write down statements from maids and compile in book form their stories. It is compelling and you almost think the people are real and not fictional characters. This was given to me by my son at Christmas. He knows the serious books I normally read so from time to time he gives me something to break up my routine. The problem with that thought was how real life this felt to me, so in effect I continued with my serious reading.

Vinie, Andy's wife read this as a member of her book club. It would be good for any book club.

Jack B. Walters
January 5, 2011

Uncle Tom's Cabin
By; Harriet Beecher Stowe

In a way I feel foolish attempting to review a book as old as this one. I have known about it most of my life but until now had never read it. It was published in 1851. It began as a serial in a monthly publication but later in book form. It was startling in its effect on the citizens of America as well as Europe. Abraham Lincoln has been quoted upon meeting Mrs. Stowe, "So this is the little lady who made this big war". It must be remembered that Europe had ended slavery many years before. Even in America the importation of slaves had been made illegal. Due to the passage of the Fugitive Slave Act, the North as well as the South was reminded that they were both responsible for the continuation of this most vile practice. She leaves no doubt on this subject as she skillfully weaves the lives of the characters into the story.

Much of what she wrote was reports of actual happenings. The net effect is in understanding the plight of the Negroes who had no recourse to their fate. We see the devastating effect of families pulled apart as they are sold to the highest bidder without thought to separating family members. We can understand that the owners were also under stress. There were compassionate owners as well as the brutal ones. The copy I just read was reprinted in 1981. It still included the ugly word "nigger". I have read recently of school boards rewriting Tom Sawyer, I can only assume they have rewritten this book as well. In my opinion that is completely wrong. That word belongs in those books. That is how it was, to pretend otherwise is stupid in my opinion and shows a lack of credibility to suggest words such as this weren't commonly used during those perilous times.

She skillfully weaved a tale using believable characters and in so doing made their plight understandable to the reader as to the depth of the suffering and pain. After years of slavery many were of mixed race but whether their skin was white or not they were still considered colored and kept in bondage. With few exceptions education was denied them. Many did become Christian. The hope of a better life in the next world was for many the only thought that was able to sustain them. Uncle Tom was completely committed to Jesus Christ and died in peace with his full acceptance of resurrection.

If you are like me and have not read this book I urge you to consider. Mine is available. I am sure it is in the Public Library as well.

Jack B. Walters
January 27, 2011

Death Clouds
On Mt. Baldy
By; Cathy Hubault

On a clear warm day November 16, 1958, six young scouts embarked on a hiking adventure to climb to the top of the tallest mountain in Southern Arizona called Old Baldy in the Santa Rita Mountain Range just South of Tucson. Three of the boys were having birthdays in November and thought this would be a perfect way to celebrate. They ranged in age from 11 to 16. This was not an officially sanctioned hike but the parents were told that it was. They were allowed to go. Others who wanted to join them were not allowed. Due to the tragic results there was more second guessing and blame spread around, none of which was of any use. Three of the boys died high up on the trail when the weather unexpectedly worsened in the early evening as they were climbing the last section, first with wind and rain and later with a heavy snowfall. Several feet fell on the mountain and six inches in Tucson which was enough to shut down the airport and make driving hazardous. Three of the younger ones gave up and returned to their base camp where they were found the next day and survived the ordeal. The other three were not found until several weeks passed after hundreds of hikers, scouts, ranchers and military personnel spent arduous days and nights trying to find and save them.

There is a permanent marker placed at Josephine Saddle near to where the bodies were found.

As an ardent hiker myself since arriving in Tucson I have climbed to the Saddle many times and on two occasions to the peak which is now named Mt. Wrightson. Every time seeing the memorial triggers conversation. Everyone it seems has a theory about it. At last month's meeting of the Southern Arizona Hiking Club the featured speaker was Cathy Hufault. She was a young girl at the time. Her younger brother was one of those that survived. On the 50th anniversary a memorial service was held. One of the speakers was her older brother. She asked him to write a story. He declined but then persuaded her to do it. She agreed and spent countless hours searching for any who had taken part in the rescue attempt as well as family members and press. It is a riveting book with the day to day events explained as garnered from her research.

As she finished her talk she told us we would have to purchase a copy of her book to understand the facts of the last hours of these boys as they tried to save themselves. I bought the book. Now I know. You should buy your own and learn for yourselves.

Jack B. Walters
January 31, 2011

Islam book reports

I decided to provide a separate section to include the many books I have read trying to understand what is happening today as militant Muslims gather strength in pushing their all or nothing agenda with astonishing effectiveness.

Islam

List of books;

_____

The Islamic AntiChrist by; Joel Richardson
Engaging the Muslim World by; Juan Cole
The Grand Jihad by; Andrew C. McCarthy
The Farhud by; Edwin Black
Honor Lost by; Norma Khouri
Cruel and Usual Punishment by; Nonie Darwish
Stolen Lives by; Malika Oufir and Michele Fitoussi
Infidel by; Ayaan Hirsi Ali
Marked for Death by; Geert Wilders
After the Prophet by; Lesley Hazelton
The Looming Tower by; Lawrence Wright

The
Islamic
AntiChrist
The shocking Truth about the real Nature of the Beast
By Joel Richardson

I was advised of this book by a like-minded friend. I ordered it from Amazon. com. The astonishing thing is that it was published and could be found for sale. The normal strategy of radical Islamics is to threaten with death for anyone writing about Mohammad or Islam in a way that they consider blasphemous. The author took a pen name and revealed as little as he could out of fear for the safety of himself and his family. The following is part of a vicious e-mail he received. It was one of many.

. . . Allahu Akhbar!! (Allah is the greatest!) Yaaaa Allah! (Oh, Allah!) I will chop off your head! May Allah damn you and your whole family. May you and your whole family rot in hell forever. I want you to know that all Muslims call upon Allah to damn you and put you in hell. I will personally kill your family. You will die a very slow and painful death inshallah (by the will of Allah) . . . .

In spite of this I will sign my name at the end of this review. When I send it out I will blind copy all those receiving it for your protection.

He tries as best he can to avoid condemning Muslims as a group. He wants us to consider them one person at a time. Regardless of his assertion, I cannot conceive that any practicing Muslim would not be offended by the premise contained in this book.

He states "This book is first and foremost a study of Islamic eschatology (end time belief) and those specific doctrines and practices that seem to correlate . . . . to the biblical descriptions and prophecies of the last days". All thru the book he quotes Chapter and verse from the Koran and from the Bible showing how similar the writings were in describing the earth's last days. He states that Muslims as well as Christians expect Jesus to return to Earth but the expectation is different for each religion.

In Chapter One he emphasizes the rapid growth of Islam. Not only Europe but also in America. Conversions from Christianity and birth rates will assure that Islam will be the dominate world religion within the next 15 to 20 years. In America the growth is predominately in the major cities. There are an estimated 350,000 in Chicago and over 700,000 in New York City. Another startling statistic is that African Americans represent 85% of conversions. He asserts that Islam will be the primary vehicle that will be used by Satan to fulfill the prophecies of the Bible about the future political/religious/military system of the Antichrist that will overwhelm the entire world just prior to the second coming of Jesus Christ. (This is pretty heavy stuff).

In explaining Islamic eschatology he states that the Qur'an mentions five things a Muslim must believe in order to be a Muslim. They are;

1- Belief in Allah
2- Belief in the last day.
3- Belief in Angels.
4- Belief in the scripture.
5- Belief in the prophets.

Christians on the other hand generally ignore the last days in spite of the fact that end-time belief plays a prominent role in the New Testament.

The principle person to emerge is referred to as Mahdi. He will be Islam's messiah. He will be the leader who will rule over the Islamic world and will lead a world revolution to establish an Islamic world order. The first order of business will be the total destruction of Israel until only a few remain. He will reign for seven years during which time Islam will be the only religion practiced on the Earth. In Chapter 5 he makes the assertion that the biblical anti Christ and the Mahdi are the same person. The prophecy also includes Jesus returning not as a Christian but Muslim converting all to Islam or having them killed. (Not a pretty picture).

Chapter 18 is a summary of comparisons between the Islamic and Biblical narrative of the end times. You will have to read to see what they are.

Whether you as a Christian believe in end times or not, a true Muslim does. This is what will drive them in their quest for world domination. My copy is available to anyone interested in pursuing further or you could order it as I did until there are no more available to purchase.

Jack B. Walters
June 10, 2010

Engaging the Muslim World
By; Juan Cole

There can be little doubt that Mr. Cole possesses a great deal of knowledge about the Middle Eastern countries including history. The purpose of his book, in my opinion, is to convince the readers that they have nothing to fear as far as Muslims are concerned.

His hatred of all things Jewish offended me the most. I readily admit that Israel together with the backing of America has pushed their weight around in their desire to provide a homeland for all of the Jewish persuasion. Jews from around the globe have migrated here as a refuge from discrimination and persecution everywhere but particularly in the Muslim world. They have successfully defended their country many times since being created in 1947. They must win or it is all over for them. This I firmly believe.

Mr. Cole, in the first chapter spells out the truth of America and England interfering in their lands in the quest for domination over their petroleum resources. These facts are well documented. I firmly believe that the wars with Iraq and Afghanistan are following the same script.

His other premise is that Muslims just want to be left in peace. He did not convince me. To be honest, I am too far gone to be persuaded that their goal is not domination of all countries on earth. If they are as peaceful as he claims why is it you can be jailed for possessing a Bible, can be killed if you convert to Christianity, why do their text books tell the students that infidels must be destroyed or made subservient to their leaders?

As I stated at the beginning Mr. Cole knows his subject. You could learn a lot about this issue by reading as long as you just add this to the information you already possess.

I want to end by quoting a comment from his Conclusion Chapter. It is on page 245, first paragraph, "If they (the Palestinians) cannot have a state of their own, then Israel will have to grant them citizenship. With one and one half million living in Israel as citizens today, this has been my personal conviction for many years. I have recommended adding small sections one at a time to allow them to be assimilated and then add more. He and I agree totally on this point.

I found this book at the public library.

Jack B. Walters
July 28, 2010

The Grand Jihad
How Islam and the Left Sabotage America
By Andrew C. McCarthy

I don't even know where to begin in reviewing this powerful book. Mr. McCarthy is another brave person who is willing to stand up and be counted. In my searching for answers over the past nine years I have read many books to try to grasp what is happening in the world and in particular America. This book in its entirety conforms to the knowledge previously gained. It is always amazing to me that writers like Mr. McCarthy can compile so much information and then share it so the reader can understand it as well.

I highly recommend reading. I found it on Amazon.com. All who seriously consider that they are patriots must learn the truth of what is happening in the world and especially in America.

There are several chapters devoted to our current president. This book asserts that he is deliberately and systematically abetting the Muslim community in their stated goal of transforming our Constitution by replacing it with Sharia law. Obama has stated over and over that America will never be at war with Islam, conveniently refusing to accept that Islam is and has been at war with America for decades. Obama has allowed these people to be infiltrated in his administration but also throughout the legal system including the Attorney General's Office, Homeland Security, the Courts and the FBI. He has ordered all agencies including the military to purge all words that might suggest the Muslim community is perpetrating acts against us. Words like; Islamic terrorists, Muslim terrorists, jihad, war, long war, global war on terror. War is now referred to as "Overseas Contingency Operation". Enemy combatants held at Guantanamo are simply referred as "individuals currently detained at Guantanamo Bay". Islam is never to be uttered in conjunction with terror. Those guilty are instead referred to as "violent extremists".

Under Islam, blasphemy is a capital offense. Anyone found guilty is to be put to death. Had the Florida Pastor burned copies of the Koran as he boasted he would do, not only would a call be put out to kill him but in my opinion the entire Muslim world would have exploded with thousands or more lives taken. There is no tolerance. How many examples do you need to hear about before you become convinced? Author Jytte Klausen wrote a scholarly book on the Danish cartoon controversy. It was to be published by the Yale University Press. It was only done after purging the guts out of the book making it meaningless. The same thing occurred to two writers in Canada, Ezra Levant and Mark Steyn. Steyn's book was entitled "America Alone". Levant's was "Shakedown", about Canada's human rights racket. In England the Cambridge University Press apologized for publishing an academic book called "Alms for Jihad". They agreed to pay damages, retrieve the books and pulp any unsold copies. A Dutch Parliamentarian after the famous cartoon drama studied the Koran and made a 15 minute film called Fitna. It recites faithfully the exhortations to violence such as Sura 9:5 that "when the sacred months have past," Muslims must "slay the idolaters wherever you find them". He was found guilty by the Amsterdam Court of Appeals for inciting hatred. Suspected al Qaeda members are welcomed in the British Parliament. Just in today's Arizona Daily Star (9/17/2010) was a very small article about a cartoonist in Seattle. Her name is Molly Norris. She had written a satirical piece called "Everybody Draw Mohammed Day". She has gone into hiding on the advice of the FBI, told to change her name and wipe away her identity. DO YOU UNDERSTAND WHAT I JUST WROTE? WE ARE TALKING ABOUT AMERICA. If I were in charge I would order the FBI to track down those who have threatened her life. It won't happen while Obama is president.

There is a complete chapter about the Enclave in Minnesota. It is a precursor of what is happening all over America including right here in Tucson. Islamicization is seeping into the classrooms where a study has been introduced called "Islam in the Classroom". The content purports how peaceful and loving the religion is. There were enough Muslims to elect a member of Congress, Keith Ellison. This is where it gets scary, the melding together of Islam and the Left. The community supported Al Franken in his successful campaign for the US Senate. Muslims find comfort and support from the Democratic Party. I wonder if the Tea Party folks are aware of this. If so, I have not heard any statements showing that they are now on the side of the angels in striving to maintain America as the founding fathers gave it to us. Perhaps a copy of this report will reach one of them and a fire gets started.

Islam is totalitarian in its designs. It would usurp almost all of what, in American society, is the secular space controlled by free people governing themselves in accordance with their own desires, under no obligation to heed any creed. This would not be possible under Sharia law. There you are either Muslim and live according to the tenants or you are dhimmis, second class citizens forced to pay tribute to your masters.

Not all Muslims share the goal of converting the world. He estimates a third are content as we are to live and work in a free society enjoying the fruits of their labor and living with neighbors who may share the faith or not. The other two thirds are divided between the violent ones who want to force the issue. There are the al Qaeda types who strap bombs to their bodies, fly planes into buildings, etc. Then there are those who are patient and are willing to devote the time and effort to conquer by infiltrating and weakening the people until their goal is reached which is the same as the violent ones.

My conclusion after absorbing the contents of this book and others I have read recently like The Muslim Anti-Christ is that the elections this November are vital. I will swallow my pride and support Republican candidates as I want Obama's presidency to weaken to where the damage he can commit is lessened. I believe he is guilty of treason and should be impeached. Many, if not all of you, will disagree with this strong statement. If I am wrong then give me your suggested books or other information for me to read which might prove me wrong. I don't think that is possible.

Jack B. Walters
September 17, 2010

THE FARHUD
By Edwin Black

Roots of the Arab-Nazi Alliance in the Holocaust

About a month ago while flipping channels on a Saturday afternoon I caught a discussion on C-Span. Mr. Black was giving his book review. It immediately caught my attention. It turned out that there were survivors of the holocaust in the audience who shared their memories with the other attendees. I went to Amazon.com and ordered a copy. I read it slowly and thoroughly over a three week period of time. The contents were so brutal and savage that it was difficult to absorb too much at one sitting.

How could it be that for thousands of years people of the Jewish faith could be persecuted as they were and as they still are today? I found it ironic that Pope Benedict XVI just this week absolved the Jewish people of the guilt of crucifying Jesus Christ. He stated that only a few Temple leaders and a small group of supporters were primarily responsible for Christ's crucifixion. Thru the centuries the Jewish people have been brutalized for this perceived sin. Had Popes taken that position centuries ago perhaps things might have been better for them.

This book primarily documents the cruelty of the Nazis and Muslims but I would be remiss if I didn't include a little about Catholics. In 1492 about 200,000 Jews in Spain were expelled for not converting to Christianity. During the Second World War the Croatia Catholics were without question the most sadistic of all time. The killing machine was called "The Ustacha". Over 100,000 Jews and Gypsies were butchered. Even the commanding German General Edmond Glaise von Horstenau reported back to Berlin ". . . the Ustachas have gone raging mad".

In his book "Mein Kampf" Adolf Hitler vilified all with a single drop of Jewish blood as being guilty and as soon as he assumed power he began the systematic removal of all Jews from Germany which culminated with the mass murder of over 6 million Jews. I found it worth reporting that the system installed to identify these victims was designed and engineered by IBM, including the Chairman Thomas J. Watson. They worked behind the scenes to bring Hitler's promises to life with great velocity and precision. I would be remiss if I did not also condemn our very own Henry Ford who was violently anti-Jewish. He published an article entitled "The International Jew and The Protocols of the Elders of Zion". Hitler proclaimed Ford as "My Hero" and reproduced thousands of copies for distribution in Germany.

In the year 610 Mohammad experienced his first revelation. At first there was a kinship with the Jews. He brought Arabs to accept "one God", the same God revered by the Jews and Christians. He sought to reinvent "God's teachings" into his unique Arab spiritualism, based not on tolerance, but destruction or subjugation of any who would not convert to Islam and Allah. The proud Jews would not convert and starting in 624 Mohammed began his campaign to kill or convert the Jews. He gave no quarter. For instance when the Jews surrendered in Medina he assembled from 600 to 900 in the marketplace and beheaded them all, taking their women as slaves. And so it began and has continued for the centuries to follow. In book 041, Number 6985 it states "The last hour would not come unless the Muslims will fight against the Jews and the Muslims would kill them until the Jews would hide themselves behind a stone or a tree and a stone or tree would say; Muslim, or the servant of Allah, there is a Jew behind me; come and slay him." (My thoughts, for President Obama to keep mouthing words to the effect that Islam is a religion of peace is a mockery of what recorded history has proved".)

For 2,600 years Jews were imbedded in the Iraqi culture as a subordinated underclass known as dhimmi. This ended in a wild killing spree June 1-2, 1941. The title of this book comes from this incident. The Arabic word for violent dispossession is Farhud. The Jews did not consider themselves Zionists but Iraqi, but after the Fahhud occurred a mass exodus began since they realized they could no longer remain in Iraq. The homes and businesses had been identified and mobs began to swarm over the city slaughtering all the Jews they could find. As an aside, British troops were stationed outside of the city limits but were not activated to intervene.

The Arab-Nazi Alliance chapter is the main subject of this book. It begins with the following statement; "Our hatred for the Jews dates from God's condemnation of them for their persecution and rejection of Isa (Jesus Christ), and their subsequent rejection later of his chosen Prophet (Mohammad) . . . Verily the word of God teaches us, and we implicitly believe this . . . for a Muslim to kill a Jew . . . ensures him an immediate entry into Heaven and into the august presence of God Almighty. What more can a Muslim want in this hard world"?

Mufti Husseini of Jerusalem met with Adolf Hitler and pledged the support of Muslims everywhere to do their part in the extermination of Jews.

He raised whole divisions trained by German officers for that purpose. This was mostly in Yugoslavia. By the end of the war very few Jews remained alive. It also occurred in North Africa. Hitler's war against the Jews stopped in 1945 when Germany was defeated by the Allies but it continued unabated in the Mid East as Jews were targeted for persecution, expropriation and expulsion after the 1948 birth of the State of Israel. The Fahrud was not a beginning, not an ending. It may not even be at a midpoint.

This last sentence was the author's book ending. I will conclude this review with my own thoughts. With the turmoil raging thru North Africa today, I am certain that as it runs its course the combined wrath of the Muslim Arabs will be directed to the accomplishment of" the final solution" by attacking Israel with the intent to eliminate the Jewish people from their part of the world. It has been documented that there are thousands of rockets placed in Lebanon, supplied by Iran. Some may have deadly tocsins as their payload. Hatred of Jews is imbedded within the Islamic faith to such a degree that I am convinced that Israel's travail may begin within months if not weeks. With Obama as our President, Israel cannot expect that America will come to its rescue. They will fight to the end. Their days of being led quietly to slaughter are over. With their nuclear arsenal they will exact severe destruction but in the end they will lose all. After that the West will be further infiltrated by those of the Muslim faith, and in the end will lose the civilization that has been nurtured for centuries, as the goal of all nations being under Sharia law is accomplished. I probably will not be alive to witness nor would I wish to be. Good luck to the rest of you.

Jack B. Walters
March 6, 2011

Honor Lost
Love and Death in Modern-Day Jordan
By; Norma Khouri

(It was later revealed that this book was written by a woman living in America. It is a fictionalized account based on facts but fiction non-the-less. I include it as it details factually government policies and tradition which I felt was important to learn about.)

This is a tragic true story written by a young woman who escaped from Jordan. Her lifelong girlfriend had been murdered by her father when he discovered she had been meeting with a man she had come to love. They had never engaged in sexual activity but just having contact with a man was sufficient to kill her by stabbing her 12 times in the chest and waiting until she was dead before calling an ambulance. As is required by law he turned himself in, was sentenced to three months in jail, was bailed out and at the end of the sentence was released for time served even though he had never spent a day in prison.

The author is devoting her life to end the age old practice in the Arab world of treating women as objects rather than equals. In Jordan's Penal Code there are two articles that allow these murders and protect the murderers. Article 340 exempts from punishment those who kill female relatives found in a situation of adultery (such as talking to a stranger). Article 98 reduces the penalty for the perpetrator of a crime when he acts "in a fit of fury" in response to a wrongful and serious act on the part of the victim. It is estimated that over 2,000 murders occur each year in Jordan and over 5,000 in Arab countries as a whole.

I am one who is always searching for knowledge. I am quick to judgment on members of the Muslim faith. What disturbed me most was that these crimes are not just committed by Muslims but also by Christians living in these countries. According to the author honor killing in Arab countries have been under Islamic Law since A.D. 644. It has been incorporated into Arab culture and is practiced by both Christians and Muslims. Christians, of course, are treated as second class citizens (dhimmah). They are required to pay a poll tax, must not harm Muslims, have any sexual engagement with Muslim women, steal the property of Muslims, nor co-operate with enemies of Islam.

In other words Christians emulate the Muslim traditions. While their women have more rights as a rule, they are still treated as unequal.

Reading this book will give you an insight on what it must be like to be a female in an Arab country, always doing the bidding of fathers, brothers and other male relatives, never being allowed to pursue whatever dreams you might have. Entire lives are spent living in fear, never knowing when you might be punished or killed for a perceived offence.

Let me close by adding my thoughts. First, I wonder why there is no condemnation by American or European women who have been so outspoken in their drive for equality in Western countries. Could it be that having achieved their goals they are insensitive to the plight of women living under Islam in countries where Islam is the law of the land. Why has our government not applied pressure for these countries to move into the 21st Century? In my paranoia I see these customs spreading rapidly throughout the civilized world. Europe in particular has been infected but I also am aware of it building in America as well and I don't like it.

As I previously stated the author has devoted her life to ending "honor killing". Read the book and find some way to express yourself to add to her efforts. Who knows, perhaps in our lifetimes these barbaric acts of hate against women could be stopped.

Jack B. Walters
September 11, 2011

Cruel and Usual Punishment
By; Nonie Darwish

Those of you who actually read my stuff understand that I have a great concern about the spread of Islam to every corner of the world. While it may be true that the vast majority do not espouse violence against those of different faiths, it is also estimated that at least 15% can be considered devout enough to commit acts of violence including death to non-believers. 15% times 1.2 billion Muslims in the world today equals 150, 000,000. I would think that any caring, thinking person would consider that many radical Muslims to be sufficient to cause alarm.

This book is clearly written and clearly understandable. Mrs. Darwish was born and lived as a Muslim in Egypt for 30 years before immigrating to America. Her mission in life is to alert Americans to the danger we face. She describes in great detail what the life of a female is like living in the Muslim world where girls as young as 9 can be married. The very thought is repugnant to me. Women are deemed to be inferior to men, not to be trusted, not to be educated or allowed any semblance of the freedoms American women take for granted.

She dissects the Koran and Sharia law and exposes the hate that drives Islamic fundamentalists to spread the curse of their "religion". I put that in parenthesis because I believe as she does that it is more a political ideology than religion. She compares it to fascism and communism, both of which are dangerous ideologies. This book is different from most in that she does offer intelligent solutions.

1- Define religion and exclude any ideology from that definition that does not pass the following test.

    A religion must be a personal choice.
    No religion should kill those who leave it.
    A religion must never order the killing and subjugation of those who choose not to be its members.
    A religion must abide by basic human rights.

2- Make Sharia an illegal law and declare it not a religion but a dangerous totalitarian ideology.

3- Control immigration from the Muslim world. Forms should clearly state that the goal of the immigrant is assimilation into democratic society.

4- Stop issuing religious visas to Muslim clerics imported from Muslim countries.

5- Ban Mosques and Muslim organizations that use religion to promote incitement to kill and hate speech against people of other faiths or atheists.

6- Demand access for access.

7- Stop shipping petrodollars to Arab countries.

8- Strengthen Western Judeo-Christian roots.

All of the above headings were fleshed out with full explanations. I cannot re-write the book for you. I can only urge you to purchase or get from your local library. Quite frankly I am pleased that a book as strong as this got published at all. I fear for the life of the author and her family. These people do not allow others to deride their prophet and his teachings.

Finally I must add that I have been concerned since our President took office with his strong support for Islam. Early on he gave a speech in Cairo that glorified the religion. We are all aware of the deep bow he gave to the King of Saudi Arabia. He has given orders to enforcement agencies not to make any reference to the Muslim religion when killings around the word happen. Two years after Ft Hood the killer is still awaiting trial. Obama considers him a radical not a Muslim carrying out a Jihad against America. That in my opinion is exactly what he did.

Now you know how I feel. I still recommend you informing yourself by reading this book and then staying alert to the danger it declares we are facing today.

Jack B. Walters
December 21, 2011

Stolen Lives
Twenty Years in a Desert Prison
By; Malika Oufir and Michele Fitoussi

This book is a true documentation based on the memory of Malika as to her life of privilege as a young girl living in the Palace. Her father was a high ranking military officer. He attempted a Coup and was shot to death. Malika, her mother and her five siblings were immediately imprisoned in a penal colony. The youngest a boy was only nine years old. After a few years they were taken to a different prison and were not even allowed to associate with each other. The conditions were harsh and food provided meager. In desperation after 15 years they were able to dig a tunnel undetected and four escaped including Malika. They were able to find responsible people to tell their story. As a result they were given a nice home and their every request was provided for except their freedom. Finally after 20 years it was granted.

This occurred in Morocco, a Muslim nation. No civilized nation would hold children responsible for the acts of a parent. I have nothing but contempt for any nation ruled by Sharia Law.

Jack B. Walters
February 18, 2012

INFIDEL
By; Ayaan Hirsi Ali

Another brave woman risks her life to challenge the authority of Muslim customs which denigrate females who are born into the Muslim culture. The vast majority are doomed to live their lives dominated by the males not only fathers and husbands but brothers and other relatives.

Ayaan was born into this life in Somalia. During her young years her family also lived in Saudi Arabia and Kenya. She did her best to learn the teachings of the Koran, attending school, reading, memorizing text and wearing burkas covering her from head to toe. As the years passed by and being exposed to other cultures particularly in Kenya she began to have doubts. She was forced into a marriage arranged by her father. He lived in Canada and had returned to Somalia looking for a "good" Muslim wife. The kind that would be obedient to him as a "good" Muslim woman should be. She was allowed to fly to Germany with the intention of continuing on to Canada but instead she entered Holland and applied for immigrant status which was granted. Her location was discovered and she had to face her husband-to-be together with older leaders trying to persuade her to marry. She did refuse and as a result was disowned by her father.

I was amazed to learn how generous the Dutch government is to immigrants. They were provided housing, food, clothes and health care for extended periods of time. The problem that developed was the refusal of immigrants of the Muslim faith to learn the language, assimilate and become productive citizens. They also sent their children to separate Muslim schools keeping them from associating with Dutch children. There were many instances of "honor" killing of girls whom became friendly with boys not of the Muslim faith. As Ayaan became more aware she began to distance herself from Islam. She learned the language, graduated from high school and went on to college. She was an avid reader trying to gain wisdom from the great authors of Europe. During these years she earned income by interpreting between the authorities and immigrants from Somalia. Many of these had to do with wives being severely beaten by their husbands. They rarely ever testified against them out of fear of being turned out of the Muslim community.

She began to speak out and over time became a sought after speaker and writer. She ran for public office and was elected. Her main goal always was to improve the lot of females. She collaborated with a film producer Theo van Gogh to produce a ten minute film depicting four punishments women could receive for various offences. It was called "Submission, Part One". There were death threats. Finally in September 2004, Theo was murdered while walking down a street. His throat was slit and a knife shoved into his chest with a warning to Ayaad that she was next. The Dutch government provided her with protection. To this day she faces death threats and has been moved to America where she continues to speak out. In March 2005 Time magazine named her one of 100 "most influential people in the world today".

Finally I want to quote from a statement she made. You can find it on page 349. "When people say that the values of Islam are compassion, tolerance, and freedom, I look at reality, at real cultures and governments, and I see that it simply isn't so. People in the West swallow this sort of thing because they have learned not to examine the religions or cultures of minorities too critically, for fear of being racist. It fascinates them that I am not afraid to do so".

I will continue to read and write reviews of books such as this. It is the least I can do.

Jack B. Walters
March 16, 2012

Marked for Death
By Geert Wilders
Islam's War against the West and Me

This is the true life story of a courageous crusader who has deliberately placed his life in danger in the hope of alerting elected officials of Western nations, including the United States, of the danger of the spread of Islam throughout the free world. It is mind boggling how they collectively, it appears, have turned a blind eye to the threat. The facts are plain to see. The Islamists have stated many times their goal of converting all nations to Islam with all the horrors that would entail. The interesting thing is that, particularly in Europe, the ordinary citizens get it but the leaders don't.

Much of the book was a rehash of the creation of Islam by Mohammad over 1,300 years ago. For me, after reading so many books on the subject, this part was redundant. Others reading this book perhaps would grasp the significance of how it all came to be.

The author proposes a suggested reason why the West has been so open to immigration from Islamic countries and why they have bent over backwards to prevent criticism of Islam. In 1973 when OPEC was formed the Western world was thrown into turmoil. That was in the middle of my working years with Firestone, so my memory is quite clear on the havoc wrought by that decision. He quotes Bat Ye'or the author of "Eurabia: The Euro-Arab Axis". He states that European Union leaders began building an alliance with the Islamic world to ensure oil supply. As part of this arrangement, Bat Ye'or contends, European leaders agreed not to hinder the spread of Islam in Europe, not to pressure Islamic immigrants to assimilate, and to ensure that European schools and media outlets would portray Islam positively. In order to accomplish this, the EU seized power over national governments. Wilders believes it is deeper than this. He contends that Cultural relativism is more to blame than oil. By this he means that immigrants need not assimilate, since that would imply the superiority of European culture over the immigrant's native cultures. Again, as I stated previously the ordinary citizens resent losing their national heritage and being forced to adopt Arab culture. The stranglehold the EU has over nations is the reason I am personally opposed to International Treaties such as the proposed Law of the Sea Treaty being debated right now in the United Nations.

Wilder's trouble with Islam dates to 2007 when he decided to produce a 15 minute documentary film about the Islamic threat. The title is Fitna. The theme was to use pages from the Koran which contain verses calling for violence, particularly against non-Muslims, with footage of terrorist attacks and other violent deeds these verses have inspired along with clips of Islamic leaders inciting violence for the sake of Allah. He states that Islam made the film, all he did was put it together. This is when death threats were made and for the past 5 years he has been living under protection by the Dutch government, sometimes being housed in prisons as the safest place to be. He was sued and for two years was under trial for being offensive to Muslims. In June 2011 he was finally acquitted because he had criticized Islam not Muslims and because he was an elected official participating in a public debate, they deemed he was entitled to greater freedom of speech than everyday citizens, that last part alone causes me problems; the thought that a politician has more rights than individuals.

He ends the book on a positive note by noting the beginnings of legislation in European countries to curb the abuses. He refuses to accept that the Islamization of the free world is inevitable. This is a valuable resource for anyone who is concerned about the spread of Islam. My copy is available to be loaned.

Jack B. Walters
August 12, 2012

After the Prophet
By Lesley Hazleton

A good friend knowing of my growing interest in all things pertaining to Islam sent me an e-mail of the author giving a talk to a large audience. Her remarks were well received. Based on that, I purchased the book.

I am not sure what I expected but what I found was a well-researched and thorough recitation of the final years of Muhammad's life and the years following as different factions vied to succeed him in authority. She brings these events to life such as you would find in a book of fiction. As a beginning student on this subject I am willing to accede that she accurately describes the events as they unfolded.

With him as he lay dying were five men each of whom over the course of time would become Caliph (successor) of Muhammad. They were two fathers-in-law, two sons-in-law and a brother-in-law. The latter was the youngest and the closet relative Ali. It would be too cumbersome for me to catalogue the succession. It is only important from the standpoint of how the split began which culminated in the division that exists even today between Sunni and Shia Muslims. In simple terms it boils down to whether sacredness inheres in the Prophet's blood family, as the Shia believe, or in the community as a whole, as the Sunnis believe.

The most compelling episode had to do with the death of Hussein in 680 at Karbala where Hussein and his loyal band of warriors were slain. He was the youngest son of Ali. It is a gripping story of courage and has since that time become a major part of the split between both factions.

She concludes by stating the mistake of President Bush in not recognizing the split and placing our forces in the untenable position of taking sides, a no win proposition. She ends by stating history is often made by the heedless, to which I enthusiastically state I agree.

Jack B. Walters
April 22, 2012

The Looming Tower
Al-Qaeda and the road to 9/11
By; Lawrence Wright

A longtime friend Glenn Puncochar advised me about this book. He knows my concern about the threat to world peace, which in my opinion, is the rapid spread of Islam into all parts of the Earth. I immediately ordered it and have been reading for three weeks. This is an outstanding effort by Mr. Wright. I can't even begin to contemplate the research necessary to accomplish such a monumental piece of work. After reading I have a much clearer understanding of how the events unfolded over the past 70 years which culminated in the destruction of the Twin Towers in New York City on 9/11.

As I have been reading and researching for the past eleven years I have learned a lot about Islam and Muslims. After 9/11 occurred I went to the Library and brought home three books about Islam. I read them and became more confused as I read any number of good things such as caring for widows and orphans and treating people with respect. As the years progressed many new books were published about how Islam really works and the evil it personifies in our present world. To name a few; "The Grand Jihad", Cruel and Usual Punishment", Marked for Death" and "Infidel", they inform the reader of the harsh reality of Islam today.

Whether you read this review or not, I am taking my time to write and it will of necessity be long. It is far too complicated to give it it's just due with just a few words. I would certainly be happy to find that a few of you would be interested enough to buy and read for yourselves. I'm not optimistic that you will.

Islam has been revised and adjusted over the centuries. Until the advent of the discovery of oil in Arab lands, these customs and practices were known only to themselves. Their barbaric treatment of women is a well-documented fact. Just this week a Pakistan father killed his 16 year old daughter by pouring acid on her. Her perceived offense was turning her head while on a bicycle to look at a boy. My oldest granddaughter turned 16 this month. She is a beautiful, intelligent young girl with a bright future. It is inconceivable to me that there exists in this world a so-called religion that supports, defends and encourages this type of behavior. They are allowed up to four wives. Osama bin Laden had as many as six and produced between 20 and 26 children according to Wikipedia. In this book, just a few months before 9/11 to took another bride. She was 15.

The purpose of this book is not to denigrate those aspects of Islam but to clearly show how violence against the West began with a few individuals who learned to hate Western culture and started the organizations that culminated in 9/11 and exist today, more capable than ever, dedicated ever more to the destruction of America, Israel and subverting Europe to their way of life.

It began in 1948 when a young man, Sayyid Qutb came to America from Egypt on a scholarship. He learned to despise American culture with, in his opinion, obsession with sex, materialism and racism. He, himself experienced racism due to his dark skin color. He said "The white man in Europe or America is our number 1 enemy. The white man crushes us underfoot while we teach our children about his civilization, his universal principles and noble objectives . . . We are endowing our children with amazement and respect for the master who tramples our honor and enslaves us. Let us instead plant the seeds of hatred, disgust and revenge in the souls of these children. Let us teach these children from the time their nails are soft that the white man is the enemy of humanity, and that they should destroy him at the first opportunity,"

Upon his return to Egypt he joined forces with Hasan al-Banna, the founder of the Muslin Brotherhood which was dedicated to convert to Sharia Law. Banna said "It is the nature of Islam to dominate, not to be dominated, to impose its law on all nations and to extend its power to the entire planet." Qutb was thrown into prison and tortured. He was hanged on August 29, 1966. His legacy continued to advance.

The next person of interest is Ayman al Zawahiri. He successfully built up a cadre of like-minded people. On October 6, 1981 followers of him assassinated Anwar Sadat, the President of Egypt. Zawahiri was captured. He was released in 1984. He emerged a hardened radical whose beliefs had been hammered into brilliant resolve.

Osama bin Laden developed into the terrorist he ultimately became. There are many pages devoted to him. It starts on page 72. We learn of his birth in January 1958. He was the son of Mohamed bin Laden's fourth wife. The 300 pages of the rest of the book chronicles his life. Early on he became a successful construction manager. After the Soviets occupied Afghanistan Osama gathered together Islamists mostly from Egypt in Pakistan to aid in the fight against the Russians. In February 1989 the Soviets withdrew. The fight now was against the Communist Party left in control. The Taliban were the primary force. They tolerated bin Laden and allowed him to stay. He joined forces with Zawahiri and created al-Qaeda whose goal is to lift the word of God and to make His religion victorious. Bin Laden stated that his hatred for America started in 1982 when America permitted the Israelis to invade Lebanon and the American fleet helped them.

As an aside, on page 149 a paragraph is devoted to the Saudi Arabia government which set out to evangelize the Islamic world, using billions of riyals at its disposal to construct hundreds of mosques around the globe. Music disappeared in the kingdom creating a joyless environment for their citizens.

At this point I have concluded that it would take too many pages to do justice to this book. Suffice it to state that bin Laden and Zawahiri are responsible for the growth and intensity of terrorist acts throughout the world. This includes the first attempt to destroy the World Towers 2/26/1993 by followers of the blind sheik, the suicide bombing of the American Embassies in Nairobi and Dar es Salaam on 8/7/1998. Also on October 12, 2000 a fishing boat approached the USS Cole and blew itself up while blasting a huge hole in the Destroyer. The culmination of their combined efforts occurred on 9/11/2001 with the destruction of the Towers and damage to the Pentagon.

It is stated on page 272 that bin Laden's goal stated in 1998 was to lure the United States into Afghanistan. Even though he has today been killed his legacy lives on. We still have Americans in that country sacrificing their lives while America is bled financially in the vain attempt to eliminate the fanatics who continue their single minded purpose of converting the world to Taliban government.

The purpose of this book and my attempt to review is that Islamic terrorism did not always exist at least to the extreme extent it now does. I consider it the greatest threat to world peace. It must be stopped somehow. No government, including our own seems to understand the threat or are willing to put forth the effort to stomp it out. This book needs to be read by persons in authority. I also recommend it to you.

Jack B. Walters
December 2, 2012

2010

2010

Listing in order by date

SB 1070—What happens now?

The Arizona Legislature has created quite a furor by passing this legislation. In the final analysis the only positive aspect will be that the subject of illegal immigration and drug smuggling has been elevated in the consciousness of those Americans who are concerned about matters such as this.

This letter is being written with a heavy heart as I am probably the only one who has it all figured out. Those who have taken offence at the heartlessness of Arizonans can rest easy for I am sad to tell you that nothing of consequence will occur. The reason I can say this is that the will of the majority has been continuously thwarted for many years now. Knowing the heavy burden we have been forced to live with we have taken every opportunity to vote for any proposition designed to stop the invasion into our State.

Several years ago we approved strong penalties against employers who knowingly hired illegal immigrants. The thinking was that if jobs were not available they would return to their own country or migrate to other parts of the country. That was callous on our part but we felt if it worked as we hoped then other States could pass their own laws to do the same thing. Over time the illegals would be squeezed out. The problem is that the law has not been enforced. The reasons given were lack of funds and higher priorities. To date only two firms have been identified. One of them had already closed their doors and no action has been taken against the second firm. Perhaps it was a mistake in the wording of the resolution in that proper funding was not included. In my opinion the answer is that those in positions to enforce just do not agree and have sat on their hands defying the will of the people.

SB 1070 with a few exceptions will not be enforced. To start with random stops are prohibited, so the advice I would give to those here illegally is to have your vehicle in good operating condition. Be sure head and tail lights are working and obey all traffic rules. If in a 25/mph construction zone, drive 22/ mph, etc. Do not give law enforcement officers an excuse to pull you over and question you as to whether you are in America legally. If you are pulled over just show your drivers license whether obtained fraudulently or legally and you will be free to go on your merry way.

It should be readily apparent that there are two sanctuary cities i.e.; Flagstaff and Tucson. Both City Councils have voted to sue the State. Whether their suits are successful or not, I ask you what directions will they pass on to the Police Chief and how hard will they come down on any officer who takes the initiative to follow the law. I think you know the answer to that. There will be a few deportations. You can be sure the Arizona Daily Star will print heart wrenching stories about families being broken up and how they just wanted to be good citizens living here whether they came legally or not.

We all know that neither political party in Washington has the fortitude to enforce laws that have been on the books for decades fearing backlash and lost votes from the Hispanic Community. There will be many sound bites but the only result, if any, will be a repeat of times past with citizenship granted to millions. Hollow threats about keeping others out will be just that, hollow threats and so America will become more Latinized on a steady trend until the majority has been attained. At that time we will be just like Mexico and the other Central American countries with corruption the rule. I of course will be long gone when that occurs which is the reason I feel compelled to make my voice heard now.

I am not totally depressed as there are a few brave souls out there trying to resolve this issue in a reasonable fashion. Perhaps in the end reason will prevail. We can only hope. In the meantime those in favor of open borders should relax and enjoy the fact that nothing will change as a result of SB1070.

Jack B. Walters
May 14, 2010

The
Hole
In our
Gospel
By Richard Stearns

I missed the discussion led by Ken Kolenbrander and Anne Donovan the day this book was discussed so I didn't hear whatever they had to say about it. Since then my good friend Ausma loaned me her copy to read. I have just finished and while it is still fresh I will attempt to state what I gleaned from it.

It was well written and clearly stated the needs of the people of the world but more importantly described how their condition could be improved if only those of us proclaiming to be Christian actually began to live as Christians. I include myself in this condemnation as there were many times in my life when I looked the other way. Without being too hard on myself I did my best to provide for my family, my company, our employees, our customers and our community. We were always active participants in our church and made contributions with treasure and talent whenever we could. I only share these thoughts as all thru the book Mr. Stearns asks us to think in terms of individuals with the sure conviction that if we did we could change the world.

There is a chapter on Time, Talent and Treasure. It matters not if we are billionaires we can make a difference. There are some at Rosemont that work in soup kitchens. Others visit the sick and offer friendship and companionship. There are many ways to help others less fortunate than ourselves.

There was a study made that is mentioned in the book. It compared the lives of people who claimed to be born again Christians and Atheists. Their behavior was very similar, much of which was not to be admired. He takes from this that words don't determine actions but good works do. He insists that faith is foremost but also that faith without good works is empty. He points out the staggering sum that could be amassed if Christians as a dedicated group would tithe and give a substantial portion to improve the lives of those less fortunate than ourselves.

I am going to close by saying that most of us consider that we are a Christian Nation. If that is so, why do we spend staggering sums on armaments of all kinds? How can this be doing Christ's work in this world? A tiny portion used properly could help to improve lives and reduce hatred among nations and religions. Our government thinks granting loans so countries can purchase arms from our protected defense industries, is being of benefit. I say no. Help dig wells, build school houses, treat the sick and show them how to be self sufficient, the benefit of that type of program would be beneficial and who knows we just might increase harmony throughout the world. Perhaps even other religions might want to participate in humanitarian programs as well.

The HOLE he refers to is the lack of carrying out God's promises. Mouthing platitudes and singing in the Choir on Sunday just isn't enough. I hope many of you will read this book and further that discussion groups probe it further.

Jack B. Walters
May 22, 2010

(I wrote this letter after reading his book "The Hole in our Gospel". He is the President of World Vision. I had sent a donation)

Dear Mr. Rich Stearns,   May 24, 2010

I fully understand the demands on your time and how every minute is precious and must be used for the maximum contribution you can make for the beneficiaries of the work being accomplished by the World Vision organization. At our church your book was encouraged to be read and discussed. I had the recent good fortune to receive unexpected funds. After learning more about achievements of World Vision I decided to share a portion in support. I will again as I feel able.

I made a special request and that was to be able to send a copy of a serious book I wrote that perhaps you or some member of your staff could check out. The book represents my thoughts on what needs to be done and isn't, with the admonition that if we don't the whole world will lose out. This was a theme I picked out from your writings. Much of my book has to do with various subjects. I have identified those of a religious nature as being important. I too have tried my whole life to learn truths. I cannot state that I have attained the level you have. What I have concluded as one of my articles states is that we are all God's children and that if that is not true then there is no truth.

1- Preface
2- My political Journey-April 2003
3- We are all God's Children-April 2003
4- Open letter to the Israeli Government-June 2003
5- What if—a look at history as it might have been-June 2003
6- This is a general letter to members of my own family and friends who sent Christmas cards to me.-February 2005
7- Jim Wallis-May 2005
8- Richard Bland—Special assistant to Jim Wallis-June 2005
9- American Empire-June 2005
10- The Season for giving-December 2005
11- While Europe Slept-August 2006
12- For the Beauty of the Earth-September 2006

We each try in our own way to make a positive difference however small.
Sincerely yours,
Jack B. Walters

No good to use Guard as paper pushers
(Published in the Arizona Daily Star on 6/1/2010)

Do you really think that Americans are happy with the decision to send troops to the border? Perhaps they are but not me. It will be no different than the last time. They are not sent as soldiers but as paper pushers. They were not allowed contact with illegals or drug runners. They were forced to back down when they encountered men with AK-47's. Their officer was quoted as saying they followed orders. Of course they were. Why not instead call out and demand the invaders drop their weapons and surrender to authority. Then the message might finally get thru that our government meant business. It will not happen I can assure you.

More letters, less Fritz
(This letter was published in the Arizona Daily Star on 6/15/2010)

I wrote it as they were filling up the editorial page with cartoons and editorial columns by David Fitzsimmons leaving minimal space for letters from people. For the record I did enjoy his walk around Tucson articles. They were informative and enjoyable. As a short term series it was OK. I only wrote when the Star gave him a large portion of the page for his political commentary which had the effect of shutting out average concerned citizens.

Is it your intention to keep reducing the space available on the editorial page so that fewer citizens' comments will be printed? Not only does Fitzsimmons have a cartoon but also a large column almost daily anymore. Some of us are growing weary with his placing us in the category of stupid and racist. I like to read articles from the people, not paid journalists.

Stupidity at the G-20 Summit

The purpose of the gathering of "leaders" from the major countries was to find a way to restore fiscal sanity. They are all awash in debt with the exception of China which has so much of the world's debt that they can't spend it fast enough.

I find it extremely ironic that the estimated cost of Security was $900 million. Protesters assemble any time these mega conferences are held no matter which major city in the world. There is much to protest about but that is another topic. I certainly hope that the Mayor of Toronto promptly bills all 20 nations to cover this cost. The good citizens of Canada should not have to pay alone.

How about this for a suggestion, hold the next meeting on the island next to Ketchikan, Alaska? This is the place where the bridge to nowhere was to be built. They could meet in the hanger. Bring in trailers for their accommodations and eat simply.

Jack B. Walters
June 28, 2010

The
Overton
Window
By; Glenn Beck

Ok, I know how you feel about Glenn Beck. I can take him sometimes and others I can't. I believe he stretches the truth to make his points. At any rate I found this book at the public library and said to myself, oh well, why not.

He weaves his general philosophy of government into a "thriller". That is how he described it. It pits the ever decreasing minority of patriots against the powers that are in control. The time is not too far in the future. Those in power are getting anxious to garner complete control over the masses who they believe will give up all pretense of being a government of the people. All that is needed is a 9/11 incident, only one more deadly, then out of fear whatever freedom still remains will be surrendered.

It is conceivable for me as I believe the mega corporations already have us under their thumb. With the vast resources available they can sway the people out of fear to vote for the candidates most beholden to them. I can see the time when they tire of the game and go for the whole enchilada.

He weaves many facts into his story and at the end provides access to web sites to learn more. This book is just presenting his views in a more casual manner.

Jack B. Walters
July 28, 2010

After Empire
The Birth of a Multipolar World
By Dilip Hiro

Whenever I see a title like this I can't resist reading. I wrote an article dated June 9, 2005 entitled American Empire by Andrew Bacevich. In it I referred to two others, After the Empire by Emmanuel Todd and The Sorrows of Empire by Chalmers Johnson. The article summed up my conclusions of all three books. This was included in My Last Angry Man book. I just recently wrote a review of The Post-American World by Fareed Zakara dated 7/19/2010. I had sent this to you by e-mail and also placed it in my blog, http://jackbwalters.blogspot.com.

This book I am reviewing was published in 2010. It takes the theme from the earlier ones and brings us up to date on where we stand as a nation at this time in his estimation. His conclusion mirrors Zakara's book which was published in 2009. Much of the earlier predictions have been proven true. Having lived through the decades where we became the strongest and best nation in my time on earth, it continues to sadden me that the decline is accelerating with a total lack of understanding by our elected leaders on what is needed to reverse the downward spiral. I am convinced it doesn't have to be this way. We need to recognize that we cannot go it alone in the years to come and we must accept that dropping bombs and sending our carrier fleets to trouble spots around the globe will no longer be acceptable to the rest of the world nor with our own people.

The tragic preemptive wars started by George W. Bush have done the greatest harm to our standing in the world. The loss of lives of our servicemen together with the lives of Iraqis and Afghans and squandering over one trillion dollars has hurt us greatly. While all of this was taking place President Bush gave away billions in tax breaks mainly benefiting the richest among us. We as a people were not asked to shoulder the financial burden, just go out and spend to keep the economy moving and leave the fighting and dying to others. At the time I felt this was disgraceful. Now that President Obama echoes this thought I haven't changed my mind.

Before I start with the review I just have to share information on page 45. He reports that a team of American experts calculated the IQs of the U.S. presidents since George Washington using a complex process. They found that George W. Bush scored poorly on "openness to experience, cognitive proclivity that encompasses unusual receptiveness to aesthetics, actions, ideas and values", a factor closely associated with intelligence. Compared to Bill Clinton (182), John F. Kennedy (182), Abraham Lincoln (195) and Thomas Jefferson (199), Bush's score was zero.

If you took the time to read my Last Angry book will know my low opinion of him. He was a disaster for America and the world. How he got thru college is beyond my ability to comprehend. There is so much I should report but the enormity of it all prevents me from condensing the book content into sound bites that might spur you to read. The sum total of it all is that America continues to extend itself militarily throughout the world and exhausting itself financially by going deeper and deeper into debt. The rubber band can only stretch so far and then it will snap. Our perceived enemies need only to wait us out while they grow stronger.

Communism is defunct now replaced by pseudo capitalistic systems that mirror capitalism but remain managed under tight control. It appears to be effective. Countries like Russia, China and India have been increasing their GDP by healthy percentages on an annual basis improving the lives of their citizens while America has floundered with stagnant growth, increasing joblessness and decline in the standard of living we had enjoyed for decades. These countries while allowing some freedom still keep a tight lid to prevent the excesses that are rampant in America as seen by the financial meltdown that has still not run its course.

Our political system has deteriorated into warfare between the major parties. Billions are spent annually swaying the voters which in the end changes nothing. No candidate has the courage to take controversial positions if not wanting to seem radical. Staying the course is the most radical position they should take. With Corporations free to spend all they wish I see no hope of getting sanity and honesty back into the system.

In his epilogue chapter he says, "By strictly regulating the appreciation of the Yuan against the dollar, China continues to sell its products at prices lower than those of American-made products". He also states, "That China and Russia will prevent the United Nations from authorizing military action against Iran, no matter what it does with its nuclear program". This means we go alone or with a few allies. A multi-polar world is taking shape. His last sentence is, "That marks the end of the American Empire".

Jack B. Walters
August 14, 2010

Farewell remarks to Pastor David and Liz—August 15, 2010

I listened to your sermon last week. You will get no cards from me. What you will get is me standing here in front of God and this congregation and telling you once again to your face, "Pastor David and Liz" I love you both.

I have apologized to you for being too familiar and friendly to you. When I say you, Liz, I want you to feel included in my comments. I know you have accepted me and have understood the great respect I have for you. It is really your fault, with that great grin on your face and your sense of humor, how could anyone not react as I have done.

How special has it been for me to stand next to you during choir rehearsal or in church on Sunday mornings. You sway back and forth and jab me with your thumb and in all ways make it special for me. I only hope the congregation accepted it as well.

I had been attending Rosemont off and on for 17 years without becoming a member. You asked me to consider it. My response was you had to accept giving me several hours of your time, one on one. I asked you to read again my two religious letters from my "Last Angry Man" book. The one was "We are all God's Children" dated April 2003 and the second "This is a general letter to members of my own family and friends who sent Christmas cards to me". This was dated February 2005. After reading and a lot of soul searching I asked if you still wanted me to join the church. You said yes and on Easter Sunday this year I did.

You have allowed me to put your name on my e-mail list which I use to forward articles I write or from other concerned friends. You not only allow me but encourage me to do so. You have even told me you have read from my books for which I am grateful. I sometimes flatter myself that I hear my words coming back to me in your sermons. Last week you made the point that America is a Christian nation. Reading the prayers of presidents like Lincoln, F.D.R., Reagan, and Kennedy how could you conclude otherwise.

Lastly, you are moving on. This is always hard to do. Most, if not all of us are truly saddened to see you go. You have rejuvenated this church (small though we may be). It has been fun to attend church as well as being a religious experience. We are sad to see you go but are thankful you will be sharing your talents at your new church in Iowa. Life is a series of steps each of us make in our lifetimes that takes us from place to place. I have often used the expression that as life progresses windows open up. We have the choice to step thru or let them pass by. Whatever the decision you make you should never look back and question your decision. You only get one choice. You have stepped thru.

Good luck, God speed, we love you, goodbye.

A wake up call for America

I am grateful that the Islamic leadership has chosen to shove our precious commitment to religious freedom down our throats. What they have done is bring out into the open their program to take over America without dropping bombs. They are using our Constitution to further their aims. They have been exceedingly successful throughout most of the world including Europe. Sharia courts are allowed to function in England right now.

The number quoted to erect this Mosque is $100,000,000. I don't know about you but that is a large sum to me. I feel proud to drop a twenty dollar bill in the collection plate on Sunday morning. Where is the investigation journalist to dig in to find out who is supplying these funds? I would venture to guess it is Saudi Arabia. It is well documented that they contribute large amounts providing Islamic education in Pakistan and Afghanistan. They are called Wahhabi madrassa and are a conservative fundamentalist offshoot of Sunni Islam and the official religion of Saudi Arabia's rulers.

In today's Star there was an article about the stoning to death of a young couple in Afghanistan found guilty of adultery by Muslim Taliban militants. It is considered legal punishment in Iran. If you follow the news you should be aware that a young woman was sentenced to die in this manner recently. It has been postponed due to condemnation from outside Iran but her fate is still in their hands.

Our so called leaders including the President and the Mayor of N.Y. are spouting religious freedom garbage. They should instead condemn this sacrilege. It boggles the mind to think that they want to build this structure at ground zero of the dastardly attack on the World Trade Center by Islamic terrorists. People like to refer to them as extremists. I think not. Just check out the atrocities others have committed over the last decade all around the world.

Again I say thanks for the wakeup call. The question is will it be heeded by those in leadership positions.

Jack B. Walters
August 17, 2010

Muslim Structure near ground zero

This is another attempt to get the attention of the editorial staff of the Arizona Daily Star about the opposition to the one hundred million dollar Muslim structure planned to be constructed near the place that used to be the World Trade Center.

It is my belief that it is an affront to all Americans or should I exclude those high and mighty all knowing who consider us bigots, racists, etc. I leave it to you to add other negative traits showing our ignorance and backwardness.

Since these people probably won't even notice I will now report on the article in today's Star from Riyadh, Saudi Arabia. It seems a supermarket had hired eleven women as clerks. Under pressure from strict religious groups the women were discharged.

When will the women of America start to speak up in defense of women all over the world who are demeaned on a continuing basis whenever Muslims are in the majority and Sharia law is enforced? A good friend who is female wrote to me and said American women would never stand for it. I replied that when that time arrived she would not have a voice in the decision.

Jack B. Walters
August 27, 2010

Teach our children the Constitution and the Bill of Rights

I feel compelled to write in response to your lengthy editorial in today's Star entitled "Ethnic-studies defense group must be open". I support your insistence that the Ethics Group clean up their act. Have any of your reporters checked into where the funding is coming from? If you did I am convinced you would realize that it is being supported by the organizations that were responsible for the Legislature passing House Bill 2281 in the first place. Check the La Raza web site as a good place to start.

Teaching Hispanic youths that the white founders of our country were evil and that white people today wish to hold them down is completely wrong. Whether America was wrong about taking the territory of New Mexico, Arizona and Southern California from Mexico is of no interest. There was a war and that was the result. The home is where families can discuss their heritage, not the schools. That goes for the children of all immigrant families whatever their race or creed.

What should be taught to all students before they reach High School is a full year curriculum about our Constitution and the men and women who placed their lives on the line to give us today the freedoms we still enjoy? That the men who wrote the words were white and wore powdered wigs does not detract from the fact that they forged the greatest government doctrine of all time, a doctrine some, I fear; believe to be outmoded and needing correction. Should it need to be improved there is a Constitutional process to accomplish that change.

I will be thankful should you be able to assure me that what I propose is already happening. Since my children have long ago attended High School I do not have information from them. I am convinced however from the attitude of students showing disrespect to speakers who do not mouth the words they want to hear, that the Constitution is not a part of all students curriculum.

Jack B. Walters
September 22, 2010

Why I am Confused

In today's Arizona Daily Star (10/3/2010) there was a recap of votes taken in Congress last week.

The House voted 348 to 79 in favor of enacting trade penalties on China (HR2378). In Arizona, Democrats were in favor and Republicans against. I have promoted this for seven years now. This vote is meaningless without the Senate also voting and the President signing into law. So now we hold our breath awaiting their return after the elections. Based on this with more Republicans in the Senate it probably won't occur anyway. Since it has been so obvious for so long that China was not playing fair why did it take until now for the House Democrats to take action? Even if the Senate had voted in favor I doubt the President would have signed the bill.

On a different bill the Senate voted 53 for and 45 against a bill (S3816) which would have rewarded companies repatriating jobs back to America and penalizing the reverse. It did not pass as 60 votes were required. Guess what McCain and Kyl both voted against. These guys are supposed to care about American jobs. This is what they do to show their concern. They keep mouthing platitudes but when the rubber hits the road they take a powder.

Somebody please explain this to me with all the talk about great Republican victories. No one is as upset as I am with the Democratic Party but as the above shows I have no respect for the Republicans either.

Jack B. Walters
October 3, 2010

Afghanistan Question

Our politicians, military officers, media and others are debating ad nausea about what steps to take to solve the riddle of this poor country that has centuries of history of being conquered by other nations. The United States with support from a few NATO countries being the latest.

I find this tragic not only for them, but also ourselves, as we continue to be trapped by an ideology that demands that we never surrender but must always be victorious. What this means is that when our current president makes his decision it will be to remain and in all likelihood involve increasing our forces. He can make no other decision. If he did he would be accused of being a coward, and a betrayer of all those who have given their lives in that country.

There is no getting away from it we are a militaristic country. We see the world conforming to our viewpoint or risk our wrath. Being a super power means only that we have the capability of destroying any and all that do not conform. Under the Republicans it was called Pax Americana. Obama was elected partly because of his disagreement with the war in Iraq. So far we still have substantial forces there with no clear cut decision to end our occupation any time soon.

Americans are divided on what course to take in both countries mainly I insist because they have no personal stake in it. Their sons and daughters do not have to die as there is not a draft which would equalize the equation between rich and poor. That is the fundamental difference when compared to Vietnam.

I started writing this article to bring to light something that I have not heard or read about. To refresh your memory, the invasion of Afghanistan was a direct result 9/11/2001 and our desire to punish the Taliban because of them allowing terrorist training camps in their country. In addition all decent persons were appalled at their stern treatment of the people. Women, in particular, were denied dignity. They could not be educated, nor could they work outside the home as nurses, teachers or anything else.

Now here is the punch line. We joined forces with a group already fighting the Taliban. They were called, "The Northern Alliance". It worked to our advantage. We gave them support including heavy weapons and air support. Our troops acted as advisors minimizing loss of American lives. It was brilliant. Why then must we now go it alone? I realize training of Afghans is in process but what happened to the Alliance? They should be fighting for their country as they did at the beginning.

It is after all, their country not ours. I am not soft on the need to control radical Muslim terrorists and the threat they pose to us, but continuing to fight and die here, if anything just enrages more to join with them to drive out foreigners as they did the Soviets.

One final point, the downfall of the Soviet Union was caused to a large degree because of the cost of fighting in this country. We face the same situation. We are nearing bankruptcy just as they were. For this reason alone we must leave this tragic part of the world and let them settle matters as they choose. Perhaps we would no longer be the object of their wrath.

Jack B. Walters
October 7, 2010

Granddaughter Robin's itinerary for her visit—Oct. 2010

Saturday-She arrives in Phoenix at 9:11 AM. I will meet her and take her to breakfast at the same great restaurant Chris and I found after his arrival. Then assuming she is up to it we will go to Sea Life Aquarium to check it out. It is in Tempe and just opened this summer. After lunch we will drive to Tucson. Roxanna will be gone this day as she will be near New Mexico climbing Owl Peak which is the last of the Coronado High Point Peaks she needs for her award.

Sunday—I plan to take her to my little church so my friends there can meet her. I had done the same with Chris. In the afternoon she will go with us to McHale Center to be part of 15,000 screaming fans as we urge our team "The Wildcats" on to victory.

Monday-This will a day of driving to the Tombstone area. It is scenic and historic. After lunch we will go to Kartcher Caverns for a tour. Chris really enjoyed it. I am sure Robin will as well.

Tuesday-We will probably go hiking in Sabino Canyon in the morning. We can do some shopping, hiking, swimming in the afternoon. In the evening it is back to McHale for another basketball game.

Wednesday-I am thinking of driving up to the top of Mt. Lemon so she can see the contrast between the low desert and the ponderosa pines on top at 9,000 ft. elevation. In the evening I have tickets for the Broadway production of Beauty and the Beast.

Thursday—We will drive to the West side of Tucson, do a little trail walking, visit the Visitor Center to see the desert video then either Old Tucson which is a restored old town with amusement rides or the Desert Museum. She can decide.

Friday—This is her day to meet my golfing friends as we play a round of golf. She gets to ride in a cart and can cheer me on as Chris did. Afterwards we go to breakfast.

Saturday—This is the day she returns home. Her plane leaves at 8:50 PM. We will leave Tucson about 4:30 PM to be sure to get her there in time. Probably won't do anything strenuous during the day. She can decide after being here a week what she would like to do.

Miscellaneous—I just wanted to give her an idea about what she will be doing. The only things locked in stone are the caverns, the Broadway show, the two basketball games and golf. Everything else can be revised. If there is an easy Hiking Club hike planned I would like her to join it and visit some of our hiking friends. I would like her to meet my friend Ursula perhaps for lunch. There will be time for resting, reading, swimming, shopping etc.

Memories of Robin's visit to Arizona
November 20 to 27, 2010

Day 1-I was concerned that something might happen to keep me from being at the airport as she walked out of the jet way so I had asked Kathie Sharp to be on tap should she be called. Fortunately I got there in good time with an hour to spare. Robin came off looking fresh and happy even though she wasn't able to sleep on the flight.

We drove to Kathie's home and Roland prepared a great breakfast of bacon, scrambled eggs, fruit and juice. Afterwards Kathie showed us her pool. Robin got excited so we returned so she could put on an old shirt then we all returned to watch her swim and also warm up in the hot tub. While she was showering we enjoyed a cup of strong coffee, then Kathie drove to Tempe so we could visit the new Sea Life Center. It was well done with many tropical fish including Sting Rays, Sea Horses and Devil Fish. Robin got to keep a fun picture as a memento. Then we went to see the Bass Pro Shop. We all thought about you Rene' and how it would have temped you. There was a large fish tank and stuffed animals all over the place. We had lunch in their restaurant. The adults had trout, which was delicious. Robin had corn dogs and apple sauce.

We returned to Kathie's, said our goodbyes and took the drive to Tucson. After an hour Robin dozed off. Nearing home we stopped at Safeway to buy STRAWBERRIES and other fruit and a box of raison brand cereal. We picked up the dogs returned home, met Roxanna, put her clothes away, ate ice cream with strawberries. Robin took a book to bed and that ended the day.

I should also add that Roxanna completed her hiking quest for the Coronado High Point Award by climbing Owl Peak which is on the border of New Mexico and Arizona. She now has achieved all of our mountain climbing awards and is working on a new category of trails in the different mountain ranges. I am doing this as well but only on ranges close to Tucson. I won't make the long car rides just to hike trails.

Day 2-We let Robin sleep in because we felt she needed it so I walked the dogs by myself. We did go to church at Rosemont community Church. I made sure she met all my friends and during the open portion I also told the entire congregation who she was, her age, and her courage in flying alone from Anchorage. Many spoke to her during the greet part of the service.

We did some grocery shopping on the way home. After lunch of pork chops we took it easy until it was time to go to the game. Our attendance for whatever reason is not as high as in past years. There were just over 12,000 people. Capacity is 14,500 which has been the norm. Robin didn't really understand what basketball was all about but she paid attention. Her lemonade helped somewhat. We played Northern Colorado and beat them easily 93 to 70. Our coach cleared the bench or our points could have been higher. We returned home for a Mexican dinner of free Tacos which a local restaurant provides anytime our team scores over 70 points. Robin started working on a project while I read. Roxanna played for an Elks club function that evening.

Robin kept saying she wanted a typewriter. I showed her Word on the computer. She started writing her thoughts on the trip which I will print off to take home. We did have our ice cream treat Rocky Road which she had selected at the store.

Day 3-Believe it or not Robin got out of bed early enough to walk the dogs with me. I took her on the two mile trail in Canyon Ranch which is just a short walk from our home. We stopped to look at the colorful Karp fish in the pond. Two deer crossed our path.

This was our day to travel to Tombstone, "The Town Too Tough to Die" We had a bowl of Chili at Big Nose Kate's Saloon. She had lemonade, I had a beer. Then we wandered along Allan St. stopping in stores. Robin bought some gifts for Chris and Arden. We also bought a slab of fudge. She had thought about bringing some home but somehow it just disappeared, sorry. She took lots of pictures to share. Amy, if you haven't already done it you should rent videos of "The Gunfight at the OK Corel". Kevin Costner was in a good one but there others as well including "My Darling Clementine" starring Henry Fonda. We drove to the "Boot Hill" cemetery. This was where Robin got carried away with picture taking which weakened the battery.

We now drove to Karchner Caverns for our 2:15 tour of the Big Room. I had remembered it as cold but it is anything but, a nice humid, warm atmosphere. Robin stayed close to the guide as Chris had done. She enjoyed it as did I. Since picture taking was not allowed I bought a few pictures for her to show her family. Then we drove home and enjoyed a spaghetti and salad dinner prepared by Roxanna. After dinner Robin continued typing her story and I went to bed early. She didn't have ice cream but did eat more fudge and drowned it with egg nog.

Day 4-I got up early to take the dogs to Kathie's home for the day. After an early breakfast Roxanna drove us to the meeting place for a Southern Arizona Hiking Club hike in the Tucson Mountains led by our great friend Jim Terlep. There were nine on the hike which was a five+ mile hike in the desert West of the Tucson Mountains. Jim handed Robin his GPS and asked her to lead which she gladly did. We had a hard time keeping up with her. The weather was perfect. We stopped at Gates Pass on the way out. This is a very scenic overlook as you approach the Tucson Mountains. Robin climbed the hill to the stone house, the same one Chris climbed to on his visit.

On the way to lunch we stopped at the U of A store to return Arden's tee shirt. I had purchased one too small which Roxanna had discovered and we replaced Robin's U of A pin that wouldn't stay closed. She and I had chocolate milk shakes for lunch. She ate macaroni and cheese and Roxanna and I had hamburgers. We picked up the dogs from Kathie's. Robin collected a few Ostrich feathers. We came home, I crashed, she typed and then at 5:30 we headed to McHale for another basketball game against Bethune-Cookman. We won again 78 to 45. It was a close game at halftime we were only up 7 points but we blew them away in the second half. Robin is really getting into the idea. She cheers and delivers insults on cue with the crowd. We came home to a late dinner of free tacos once again and chicken strips followed by ice cream and cake.

Day 5—Robin woke up at 6:00 so I didn't have to wake her. After breakfast we went to Dorado Golf Course to meet my friends Pat and Doug for a round of golf. She ran all over the course, collected oranges, grapefruit and blossoms. She helped holding the flag pole and sometimes pulled my cart. We had to keep warning her to stay behind us as we were hitting. Pat won as usual; Doug beat me by a stroke by paring the 18th hole. Then we went for breakfast. Pat's wife Sandy joined us. We had our usual fun conversation spiced because of Robin's input. She learned a golf joke. You ask a golfer what is his favorite day to play golf. The answer is any day that ends in a y.

After we returned Roxanna took her to our pool complex. She squealed when she stepped in the cold water so she just warmed up in the hot tub. Then Roxanna took her to the Visitor Center at Sabino Canyon and then a hike to the Dam and other trails. This was partly for me to have nap time so I wouldn't fall asleep during Beauty and the Beast. We were in row U which was fine but Robin did watch most of it thru binoculars. It contained beautiful music, great voices, spectacular costumes and scenery. It lasted nearly three hours. Robin slept on the ride home. She insists she just had her eyes closed. At any rate, we let her sleep in until 9:00 Thursday morning.

Day 6-We were out of fruit so I went shopping for strawberries, blueberries, bananas, milk and juice. Robin ate a whole container all by herself. Roxanna made us scrambled eggs. Then Robin and I took the dogs out, this time we went thru the streets. She saw Gamble Quail. Came home, played on the computer, watched a little of the Macy's Parade. We left for the Birger's home about 2:00 for Thanksgiving Dinner. Judy and Jim Marvel were there. We enjoyed a sumptuous meal. Jim informed s of the good news that Jana is pregnant at age 38. She and Vince have been trying for years now so this is really quite exciting. She is receiving great care so all are optimistic of success. As usual after a heavy meal I came home useless. After typing in her report Robin is watching a Charlie Brown move about the Mayflower.

Day 7-Roxanna went on a hike to the Sonoita area. Robin and I took the dogs to Kathie's then drove east to hike "A" Mtn. It is not a true mountain but is a fun hike. Years ago a large A was placed near the top in recognition of the University of Arizona sports program. It is just west of I-10. There were 10 hikers in all. They all enjoyed meeting Robin. Afterwards she and I stopped for a doughnut to tide us over until lunch time, and then we drove to the Desert Museum and enjoyed the experience for nearly three hours. We ate lunch there, and then returned home. At 4:30 we went across the street to our neighbor and friend Joe Rein. He made us chocolate, banana smoothies. Amy, you should buy the packets and make for your family. It is really tasty. He had placed books on a table for Robin to sort thru. She only wanted one. I took two others that I hoped Chris might enjoy. We came home, had left over turkey for dinner, watched our football team lose to Oregon and later watched our basketball team win over Santa Clara in Las Vegas. Robin went to bed at halftime, another full day.

Day 8-Robin slept in until 7:30. She finished up the rest of the fruit we had bought for her. We walked the dogs, came back and lounged around while Roxanna did laundry and started getting her bag ready.

Thanks for sharing your lovely daughter with us. She has been delightful. She got compliments from all who met her.

Love,
Grandpa

Robins' notes to remember her visit to Tucson-November 2010

Kundy slobbers all over me. Boomer does not slobber on me. Boomer and Kundy are dogs. Boomer weighs 50 pounds Kundy weighs about 100 pounds. I missed walking the dogs because I was still sleeping. When I woke up grandpa told me he had already walked the dogs I was unhappy. The dogs missed me. I could tell because they whimpered at me. I hope I get to walk them tomorrow. I went outside with the dogs, they only like to stay outside for a little while outside there are some nice plants a tree, some cactuses including the old man's hair cactus that mom sent grandpa she said, that's the meet the cat she is very shy. I hope she gets to know me. My room is nice and tidy not with scorpions like Chris said. Now it is eleven thirty. I will see what happens tomorrow. I finally got to walk the dogs. I walked Kundy, he would not stop sniffing every bush we passed along with peeing everywhere another dog had peed. I had to pull him away from every bush and shrub. Boomer on the other hand only pulls ahead he follows grandpa's instructions. We hiked two mile loop Kundy and boomer were good do the rest of the way. Kundy was lagging behind. We came to a nice pond with fish in it. When we got back to the house, we got our water bottles. I got my camera and we left. We were going to Karchner caverns and tombstone hen we went back to the house we had spaghetti and salad yummy, Chris I don't know why you don't like it. After words I had a cookie, eggnog and fudge. Now lets get back to the dogs I hope you like this part of my story. Kundy is a brown lab, boomer well I really don't know for instance his colors are a mixture of orange, brown and white. Boomer has a stub of a tail; Kundy has a long brown tail, which is always in the way. Boomer has been here a shorter time than Kundy. Kundy has been here longer. Tomorrow I am going to hike, go to a basketball game and hopefully go swimming. Roxanna is playing her Accordion she is playing Jewish music I like the sound of it, it is a nice instrument she has been mostly playing Christmas songs. [Tuesday] I woke up early this morning. I had some cereal with strawberries. After words we went hiking it was five miles in all. When we were finished with the hike we ate at a café for lunch and then we picked up the dogs at Kathys and went home. Later we will go to a basketball game, go cats yesterday at Tombstone we ate lunch at Big Nose Kate, me and grandpa had chili then we left. After that we just browsed for things, I got Arden a bead bracelet and a scorpion in a glass circle. I got Chris some fool's gold I still need to get him one more thing. I got both of them nice tee shirts at the gift shop when I was going to the basketball game on Sunday. Remember go cats. Grandpa said I might be able to go swimming today, I hope so. We are going to the game at seven o'clock. Nice shot buddy. Grandpa is taking a nap in his bed. I found peacock feathers at Kathy's and Roxanna put them in a vase; they look pretty in the vase. [THANKS ROXANNA] Tomorrow I will go golfing and go see beauty and the beast the musical.

[Wednesday] the basketball game was Arizona cats vs. Bethune Cookman. Arizona scored 75 Cookman 45. We are now going to talk about the Dogs. We have not walked the dogs in two days they need exercise very badly. I think we will walk them tomorrow; I always walk Kundy its tough because he always lags behind to smell every bush and shrub. The animals I have seen so far are 2 deer, 4 quall, 1 rabbit, 2 humming birds and 3 coyote we are now going golfing. There were 18 golf spots we did all 18, Pat won 1st place, grandpa won 2nd and Doug won 3rd place. After that we ate a late breakfast with Pat, Doug, and Sandy and then we went home. Then I went swimming and went to Sabino Canyon with Roxanna. Then we came home and had spaghetti with salad [YUMMY—THANKS ROXANNA] [THANKS GRANDPA] now we are going to Broadway to see Beauty and the Beast [the musical]. At golf I fed the ducks chex mix they liked it.

[THURSDAY] I woke up at 9:00 and I and Grandpa walked the Dogs I walked Kundy and Grandpa walked Boomer. While Roxanna stayed home. Kundy peed 17 times, Boomer peed 1 time. At 2 o'clock we went to thanks giving dinner at Denise's [Jim and Judy said hi] I played with the Cat's. It is 6 nineteen Pm. Tomorrow we will hike A mountain and go to the desert museum. Today I hiked a mountain and went to the desert museum. We had the air conditioning on all week.

[SATURDAY] I LOVE MOM.

The Green President

I watched a commentary news program yesterday. The subject was green energy, which has always been important to me. The comment was made that Obama should be called the green president not the black president because of his strong commitment to green energy. They stressed the importance of wind and solar. Then they glossed over the fact that most of the jobs created to produce the materials necessary to accomplish were being manufactured in China.

I can remember during the campaign that often Obama would laud the ability of American workers and further it was assumed without question that green jobs would be created in America. I consider this a betrayal on his and Congress's part of American workers. He and Geithner continue to talk tough with China about their unfair trade policies but don't have the intestinal fortitude to take action. In the meantime they can find funds to fight obesity with their gift of $15 million to Pima County. Whoopee.

Jack B. Walters
October 20, 2010

American Conspiracies
By Jesse Ventura

I learned about this book from an e-mail I received. It intrigued me enough to purchase. I have not been disappointed. A large portion of it was confirmation of information I had absorbed over time from books read or by other means.

My skepticism began about the time of the slaying of President Kennedy. His death profoundly affected me. As he was growing in stature as president Americans began to believe in themselves again. There was hope and optimism not only here but around the globe. When news came of his death I was working in Canada. My fellow employees were as devastated as I was. Tears were flowing. I was convinced then and I am still convinced that there was a conspiracy involved not just a lunatic loner.

President Kennedy was planning to reduce our advisors in Vietnam which would have restricted the growth of the military/ industrial alliance, former President Eisenhower warned the nation about. His brother Bob was putting the heat on the Mafia without the support of J. Edgar Hoover. The CIA was playing dirty tricks in Cuba including assassination attempts on the life of Fidel Castro, at the same time Kennedy was considering normalizing relations. He was beginning to take monetary control away from the Federal Reserve. In short there were multiple groups who wanted him out of the way. With his death the hopes and dreams died with him. This book implies a conspiracy and formulates how it may have occurred. The most devastating part is the alleged cover up perpetrated by the FBI and others in authority and the fallacy of the findings of the Warren Commission.

He covers other conspiracies starting with Abraham Lincoln. I was newly aware; as this was documented for me in a Lincoln book I had just finished reading. He covers the deaths of Robert Kennedy and suggests that the assassin was either drugged or the victim of brain washing and states that the number of bullets fired could not have come from the same weapon. Here again evidence was lost or destroyed.

He raises questions about the Jonestown Massacre which are intriguing.

There are 14 chapters in all. In the later ones he comes down hard on the elections of 2000 and 2004. He insists they were rigged and stolen by various means. I agree totally. It was unbelievable that the Supreme Court would bestow upon themselves the authority of declaring a candidate elected in the middle of the vote count. In 2004 exit polls declared Kerry winning easily in Ohio but the results were just the opposite. He claims the electronic voting machines were the reason. Whether it is true or not, I continue to support paper ballots as the only sure way to prevent fraud.

Those of us who continue to believe that the World Trade Centers could not possibly be brought down in ashes within minutes by the jet fuel of airplanes are considered hopeless. Most cannot believe that government could be involved. He brings to light many factors which are inconsistent with the report of the 9/11 Commission. A cover up is implied. He condemns corporate controlled media for swaying the public.

Chapter 13 is entitled "The Wall Street Conspiracy". His condemnation of the fat cat financial gurus is right on the mark. They operated recklessly knowing full well the government would rescue them if things went wrong. He solidifies my thinking that all of Washington is in bed with these thieves and that our only hope as a free country is to vote all of these elites out of office. He and I condemn both parties equally. There is not much time left for us if this is not done.

The last chapter should be of concern. It covers the continuing loss of privacy of us all and the threat that poses on us continuing as a free people.

Whether you agree with him or not, should you take the time to read you will not be bored. Ventura's book reminds me of Lee Iacocca's book "Where have all the leaders gone". Neither author is timid about naming names and placing blame. My copy is available for anyone who asks.

Jack B. Walters
November 2, 2010

Don't give Obama credit

Large headlines in today's Star proclaim, "US will quit Iraq". The size of the print was only about half that used when Mike Stoops was fired but that is another issue. Obama doesn't deserve credit. He, Hillary and other top ranking officials have done everything they could to convince the leaders of Iraq that as many as 5000 troops should be allowed to stay after this year indefinitely. Iraq would not allow immunity and so he was forced to order bringing them home. The question remains on the size of armed contractors who will remain. To me it is just a sham to relieve concerns of those Americans like me who didn't want to attack Iraq in the first place.

Jack B. Walters
December 1, 2010

Inside Job

A documentary by Charles Ferguson is now playing at the Loft Theatre in Tucson. This theatre shows off beat films. I can only hope that it is showing in other theatres around the country so that some of you receiving this report may have the opportunity to see it for yourself. It is not new information but is put together in convincing fashion to enable the viewer to grasp the complexity of the upheaval in our financial institutions.

One of my articles in my last book was entitled "The Golden Age of America". It covered the decades following the Second World War until the mid 70's. I listed many issues leading to the good times coming to an end. I blamed the financial institutions and the mega-corporations for abandoning Americans as they strove for greater profits for themselves. This film clearly documents the demise of regulation in favor of self-regulation which was supposed to happen but didn't. It all started with President Reagan with his push for deregulation of banking, utilities, airlines, etc. All the following presidents added to the process up to and including President Obama. All thru his campaigning he talked about ending the greed of Wall St. but surrounded himself with those who were largely responsible for creating the problem. I will give him credit for knowing what needed to be done but in the end he caved in to his advisors and Congress. The bill passed was too weak to be effective. I am sure his current decision to extend the tax breaks for the very rich was due to pressure from those same advisors. One memorable statistic stated that the top 1% of Americans now owns 23% of GNP.

Both political parties are responsible which leaves us hanging as to what needs to be done. I am repeating myself from other messages I have sent out but I am convinced the politicians will continue to allow this pillaging to continue unless we find the will to resist forcibly.

Jack B. Walters
December 13, 2010

2011

2011

Listing in order by date

30 U.S. Senate votes tomorrow to force China to allow their currency (the YUAN) to float to its true value-October 5

31 Congratulations Mr. Cain-November 3

32 Why don't they get it?-November 4

33 Herman Cain may quit his Presidential campaign-December 3

34 Your editorial today, Dems, GOP need to come together on payroll tax cut-December 4

35 Revenge of the Electric Car-a documentary film-December 14

Actions Speak Louder Than Words

(President Obama spoke at the memorial for those who died in Tucson while attending a political rally for Representative Gabrielle Giffords)

At the memorial service there were many wonderful words spoken about the dead, wounded, hospital care givers, heroes and Arizonans in general. President Obama could not have done a better job, in my opinion, others may disagree. I voted for him but have been appalled at the agenda he has pushed since his election. The America I want is one where families are able to support themselves by their labor, not exist as wards of the state.

Now that the world has seen for themselves the type of people we really are, they should realize that we are not racist, hardnosed, uncaring. We have taken quite a beating since he became president. He has spoken to warn people from visiting because it is unsafe; he has turned the Attorney General loose to take our State to court over SB 1070, the employer sanction law and just recently our vote to ensure secret ballots for workers in union elections. He seems to be doing all he can to punish us for our alleged sins.

Real healing could begin if he called off the lawyers and allowed us to function as the citizens of this great State deem necessary. As strapped as our State is for funds we have been forced to spend millions defending our laws from Obama. So there you have it, like Reagan said to Gorbachev "tear down this wall", I ask President Obama "to call off your dogs".

Jack B. Walters
January 17, 2011

Here we go again

Do any of you remember the case of the two beltway snipers in 2003? What should have been a slam duck case dragged out for months. It cost taxpayers millions and then of course there were appeals afterwards. They started their killing spree here in Tucson at the Fred Enke Golf Course.

Jared Lee Loughner has just pled not guilty. He did his dastardly deed in front of scores of witnesses. He was caught on Safeway's video surveillance cameras. He deserves the death penalty but it will never happen as he will plead temporary insanity. After rehabilitation he will be released into the population to be free to do it again as the mood strikes him.

There were 250 FBI agents assigned to the case. There were instantly hundreds of local law enforcement and medical staff who responded. The stores were closed for a week while the crime scene was searched for clues. The President and many others flew in to attend the Memorial Service. Undoubtedly millions have already been spent. High paid lawyers will reap their financial rewards, all at tax payer expense. Is it any wonder our nation is on the brink of bankruptcy? This case will drag on week after week creating more headlines for our news media to exploit and costing millions.

The irony is that it was deemed too costly to assign a law enforcement officer to be on hand for Gifford's event.

Jack B. Walters
January 25, 2011

Mrs. Ellen F. Donohoe   February 9, 2011
Executive Director of the Founders Campaign
32 East College Street
Hillsdale, MI
49242

Dear Ellen,

I presume to write to you on a first name basis since that is how we addressed each other at Mimi's this past Tuesday. I thoroughly enjoyed meeting you and having a chance to exchange thoughts on a number of issues. I believe we are generally on the same wave length with a few exceptions. One of those was my affection for FDR which began in my childhood. I was 13 on Pearl Harbor Day.

I promised I would read the two books you gave me written by your Professor Burton Folsom, Jr. I am an ardent reader of history and the people who made a difference with their lives. In the book I gave you "Still Angry" there is a book review about FDR's life written by Jean Edward Smith 11/23/07. It chronicled in great detail the events of his life and in particular the programs he initiated. Just reading the intro to "New Deal or Raw Deal" tells me that as always there are two sides to every argument. Whatever I will glean from reading cannot change the fact that FDR was re-elected four times by ever increasing amounts. The American people could not even contemplate having someone else in charge during those perilous years. If your professor's conclusion is that American's just didn't understand and voted in ignorance then I will take issue with him.

Looking thru my book I want to point out another article that pertains to FDR. It is FDR's Democrats VS Today's Breed 1/26/10. Another one I hope you will read is The Golden Age of America 6/25/09. Then there are two relating to elections; "There is only one answer 9/25/08 and Election Primary is not working 9/8/08. Of course, all my writings are important or I wouldn't have written and paid the price to publish.

As we spoke I mentioned that one goal of mine was to stimulate discussion and thinking. You will find Liberal and Conservative thoughts intermingled. Only the dogmatic types stick to their basic platform without bending. My basic beliefs are simple. I believe each of us should do our very best with our lives and only accept handouts when absolutely necessary to sustain lives. Our nation today is severely divided between those who have most of the wealth and those who are conditioned to live on the largess of the government. The middle class is nearly extinct and they in my working life represented all that was the best about America.

I will stop at this point as I didn't intend to write another book in these pages. I will share that as a direct result of our meeting I have mailed a contribution to your Founders Campaign. It was for $1,000, not much when compared to Hillsdale's needs, but all I am willing to invest at this time. I have also taken the liberty of mailing under separate cover my other two books; "The Life and Times of Jack B. Walters" and "The Last Angry Man". Should you be willing to place copies of any or all in your library I would have additional sent to the address of your call without charge. Different points of view are always valuable.

Sincerely yours,

Jack B. Walters
February 9, 2011

NATO Attack on Libya

I wrote a letter the day the action started. You did not see fit to publish so I am trying again.

Letter to the Editor

The ultimate reason stated over and over is to prevent an imminent humanitarian crisis. I have a question what is the difference between Libya and Darfur? In Darfur millions were displaced from their homes by raiding bands of Muslim Arabs who wiped out Christian black villages killing and enslaving. The United Nations and NATO were reluctant to intervene when in my opinion a few drone aircraft blowing away a few of these groups might have stopped the massacre. There is only one answer I can think of, and that is "OIL". Interfering in Yemen might have disrupted the flow of oil to China and the disruption of oil to Europe from Libya is causing problems there plus raising the cost worldwide. So there you have it, oil is the answer not humanitarianism.

Also noted is that the majority of Americans support bombing Libya, how sad.

Jack B. Walters
March 24, 2011

Dear Mrs. Ellen Donohoe,   March 26, 2011

This is a letter from your new friend in Tucson. I did as requested. I read both books you gave me. The attachment to this e-mail is my sincere response. It took me five pages and several weeks of thinking before I completed it. I hope it doesn't brand me as a heretic as far as Hillsdale College beliefs are concerned. In the note I included with my other two books I asked that different points of view should be allowed to be expressed.

If you did indeed have the time to read my thoughts you realize that I am all over the lot. I don't wish to be branded a Liberal or Conservative. The problem with labels is that it forces people to stand firm without allowing for compromise which is why it is nearly impossible for government to function today. There aren't any issues that couldn't be resolved if thoughtful debate was allowed to occur.

I am using e-mail as the quickest and easiest way to send my book report. I am asking a personal favor. I would like Professor Folsom to receive a copy. Perhaps he might be interested in reading my books. I reacted strongly against his conclusions. That doesn't mean I don't respect him nor in any way mean to disparage his efforts. It is just that Roosevelt was loved by me, my family and all the people I knew during the war years. I will go to my grave still believing he was a great man and a great President.

Sincerely yours,
Jack Walters

Chinese leaders could not be happier

Every time we drop a guided bomb on a truck or tank in Libya they smile, knowing that is more wasted money being spent by America as we go further down the drain toward bankruptcy.

While Boehner and Reed huddle together trying to find agreement on which domestic program to cut the saga continues as we exhaust ourselves spending on our foolish wars in the Mid East. Case in point, in an article this morning we learn that there is an agency with 1,900 employees dedicated to finding solutions to prevent deaths from roadside bombs. They have spent nearly 17 billion to date with no results. The death and wounded numbers have increased from 270 in 2008 to 3,366 in 2010.

Here is a novel idea. Bring our people home from this cursed region. If we did that there would be no more deaths of our soldiers.

Jack B. Walters
March 27, 2011

Dear Sir,

This will be one of the few letters of support I assume, you will receive in regard to your Flat Tax proposal. I, of course, do not have the inside information to determine if 2.1% is the proper number, but I have long supported the concept. Just by taking the time to look at a tax form whether Federal or State should convince any serious person that they are riddled with a myriad of loopholes, all placed I am sure with the best of intentions to aid one group or another.

In the 80's I accepted a position as Director of General Services for the State of Iowa. I tried to convince the Governor and the Director of revenue that the State tax should be simplified. I shared copies of my personal tax forms from the years I lived in Canada as a manager of a Firestone plant. Quite simply after figuring out your taxes owed there was a multiplier line near the end of the form to determine how much would go to the Province, or in our case State. It was different for each Province and subject to change as needed. The point is that this was not additional tax but a portion to go to the Province. No separate form was required. What I had proposed was to do the same in Iowa which could be done very simply by enclosing a copy of your Federal form and multiplying the State tax owed as you had proposed.

One benefit would be the immediate reduction in the staff of the Dept. of Revenue. Those people who now open and review the returns would no longer be needed. Any time State employees can be reduced should be welcome.

When Steve Forbes proposed a flat tax for the Federal government I was in favor. As I recall he had a threshold which would have exempted $35,000 or thereabouts. Even this year at the opening of Congress there was discussion about simplifying the tax code. There is only one word to describe the code and that is abominable.

While I like the idea that everyone pays some amount to be part of this great country. Maybe the only way you can succeed is to exempt the lowest income groups. If that is what it takes then I support.

It is interesting to me that the Democratic representatives are using this to blast the Republicans and no doubt will encourage throwing out members like you. It is so tragic to me that this must be continuous warfare. The editorial writers at the Arizona Daily Star have certainly labeled you and your colleagues. Reading the letters to the editor today must make them extremely happy.

My hope is that you do not walk away from this and thru education and other means strive to overcome the bad press.

One final thought, supposedly the richest among us would have their taxes reduced by large amounts. That I believe is a falsehood. Tax shelters abound of every conceivable kind to protect the earnings of the rich. Having a tax deduction for a half million dollar mortgage is one example. I don't own a home. Many have paid off their mortgages, many others rent. There are no tax breaks for these people.

Good luck, don't despair,
Jack B. Walters

Government Shutdown Looms

Neither party is serious about the deficit.

Here is a thought which so far has eluded them; the current cost of supporting the war in Afghanistan is $2 billion/week or $104 billion/ year. Add to that the cost of Iraq and Libya plus our permanent bases in the Middle East I am sure the above cost could be doubled or more.

In addition, military aid given to many countries out of money we don't have but must borrow from China makes absolutely no sense whatsoever.

No politician has the courage or the good sense to suggest the above as they would be labeled weak on defense. What a joke. These adventures which cannot be funded are destroying the solvency of America. Who will come to aid us when our currency is worthless?

Jack B. Walters
April 6, 2011

Water for Elephants
By: Sara Gruen

My son asked me to take a break from the heavy reading I usually do and recommended this book. I just finished it. It was well done and quite interesting. I particularly enjoyed the ending. It is what we all hope could happen for each of us and that is to find some good reason to be of use to the world rather than just exist.

My father told us stories about his experiences with a traveling Carnival when he was a young man. Remembering those and melding them into this story of Circus life aided greatly in my enjoyment of reading.

This is the story of a young man studying to be a veterinarian, following his father's profession and a family tragedy that ends his life as he knew it and by accident he finds himself on a Circus train. From there the rest of the story is about his experiences. There is tragedy, love and hate abounding interwoven as all good stories should be.

I recommend reading as does the Los Angeles Times, the Wall Street Journal. Newsday Favorite Book and USA Today. It is also currently in a theatre near you.

Jack B. Walters
May 8, 2011

A Counter Proposition

President Obama is urging Israel to give up all the territory they acquired during the war in 1967 with Egypt, Jordan and Syria. This war was the third time Arab nations had attempted to eliminate the Jewish state. The forces were gathering. The United Nations Peacekeepers were told to leave. Shipping lanes critical for Israel's survival were closed. In desperation all civilian men were recalled to active service and Israel attacked first. Gaza, the West Bank, the Golan Heights and the Sinai Peninsula as well as Jerusalem became a part of Israel. Later the Sinai was returned to Egypt but the rest were kept.

Anyone with an ounce of sense looking at the borders that existed before the war would recognize that the country was vulnerable to attack. Only the skill and determination of the Israeli citizens averted a tragedy. Don't think for a moment that the Jews would not be slaughtered if overrun. Each war that has been thrust on them amounted to survival. Technology has advanced considerably since 1967. In my opinion a sudden strike would be devastating. As the nation suffered, I also believe I can state that the nations attacking would also be destroyed by the nuclear arsenal that Israel possesses.

Israel does not want this and therefore have rejected the proposition of President Obama. Israel will also never negotiate with terrorists as Hamas has proven to be over the decades.

I have a thought to share with our President. To show his sincerity I believe he should propose returning Texas, New Mexico, Arizona and Southern California back to Mexico. After all, these territories were taken from Mexico when they were considerably weaker than America. What is right for the goose should also be right for the gander, as the old saying goes.

Jack B. Walters
May 20, 2011

Coronado Forest Closing

Because of fire hazards all activity has been banned, even including our own very special Sabino Canyon. While it may be true that careless campers were responsible for some of the fires what is basically true is that average citizens who venture forth to enjoy our spectacular forest scenery are respectful of the forests.

The reality is that Arizona citizens will obey the order and stay out not because of fines but because of concern. Those entering our State illegally whether looking for work or bringing in drugs will not pay heed to this order.

The article in the headlines only suggested this at the very end of the report as if it was merely a slight possibility. Wake up, this is the problem. The closure notice will not decrease the ongoing invasion.

There I said it. Sure be nice if the Star editorial staff would identify the real problem.

Jack B. Walters
June 7, 2011

TOO BIG TO FAIL
By Andrew Ross Sorkin

I am always astounded after reading a book like this. The research involved and the time consumed appear monumental to me. I purchased the book and read it during my plane rides to visit family and friends. The author describes in incredible detail the events and conversations of the principal participants during the financial crisis in the Fall of 2008 which led to Congress approving $700 Billion in aid to the major financial institutions in what was referred to as TARP (Trouble Asset Relief Program).

This is not a book highly recommended to read except for people like me who seem to enjoy delving into issues. It is 555 pages of financial topics way over my head. I cannot even conceive of the magnitude of dollars involved.

The Cast of Characters is located at the beginning. It takes eight pages to list them all, a who's who of those at or near the top of the largest Corporations in the world. During the book the incredible sums of money are disclosed, again in amounts unimaginable to people like me.

The root cause was the irresponsible bundling together of mortgages, millions of which were given to people without the means to pay, many without a down payment of any kind. The underlining reason was the idea that housing would always increase in value. In my opinion this was idiotic. When values started dropping in 2006, people started walking away from their homes when the market value became less than the mortgage. Also during these years, good paying jobs were lost. Mortgage payments could not be made. As all of this started accelerating, the losses to the financial institutions built to unsustainable levels. Out of concern investors demanded the return of their capital. The value of bank stocks plummeted. Before the carnage was stopped by TARP, Lehman Brothers went bankrupt and was put out of business. Others like Bear Sterns, Wachovia and Merrill lynch were absorbed by larger firms. AIG was so far gone that it took $185 Billion to keep them from failing before it was all over.

"Hank" Paulson was Secretary of the Treasury; Tim Geithner was President of the Federal Reserve System. These were the two most important persons responsible for rescuing the banks. As the drama unfolded they tried to have the institutions themselves solve the problem by supporting their competitors. When it became obvious that this could not be accomplished then they pushed for government money, referred to by people like me as "bailout". TARP was originally meant to be used to purchase toxic assets. In the end all the major companies agreed to accept government funds while granting stock as collateral. The following was not in the book, but from sources available to me all loans have been paid back with interest. That would seem to give credit to those involved. My concern is that nothing substantial has been done to lessen the threat of another crisis. Legislation put forth has been watered down to where meaningful safeguards have not been enacted. Senator Bernie Sanders of Vermont introduced a bill entitled "Too Big to Fail, Too Big to Exist". Senators Maria Cantrell of Washington and John McCain of Arizona introduced a bill to re-instate Glass-Steagall. Neither passed based on the argument that we would be less competitive in the global marketplace. There just has to be a way to keep foreign banks from absorbing American owned, while still putting safeguards into the system.

The last sentence states "This generation of Wall Street CEOs could be the ones to forfeit America's trust. When the history of the Great Depression is written, they can be singled out as the bonus babies who were so shortsighted that they put the economy at risk and contributed to the destruction of their own companies".

Jack B. Walters
June 27, 2011

NATO's military mission is over

A short history

NATO (North Atlantic Treaty Organization) was created in 1949 by President Truman and 11 other countries; England, Iceland, France, Luxemburg, Belgium, Canada, Portugal, Italy, Norway, Denmark and Netherlands. It was deemed necessary to prevent Russia from taking control of Europe. The overriding mission stated that an attack on one would be considered an attack on all.

Major bases were located in France. West Germany was allowed to join in 1955. Dissention led France to gradually separate. A complete break occurred in 1966. All bases in France were closed, most of which were re-located to West Germany. By 1979 Tactical Nuclear missiles were installed capable of destroying Russian tank formations. They included GLCM and Pershing II missiles. East Germany was re-united with the West in 1990. An agreement with Russia mandated reductions in forces on both sides. NATO forces were not to be deployed in East Germany. NATO did so anyway.

With the end of the Cold War in 1991 NATO was extended into Eastern Bloc countries, one at a time which caused unease with Russia. France rejoined NATO in 1995 and attained full membership by 2009. In the ensuing years more Eastern nations have joined. A missile base scheduled for installation in Poland under President Bush was halted by President Obama lessening the threat of military action by Russia against Poland.

Where NATO is today

In June 2011 Secretary of Defense Gates scolded the members for not contributing their full effort in the bombing of Libya. He threatened that this could be the end of NATO. Only eight of the 28 member States contributed forces to the Libya campaign. They were America, England, Canada, Germany, Poland, Spain, Netherlands and Turkey. Gates was critical of Poland, Spain, Norway, Turkey and Germany. Norway is ending operations August 1, 2011. The British Navy has stated operations are not sustainable and the Danes have run out of bombs. How ridiculous is this. What it means to me is that NATO is a hollow shell militarily, only held together by the might and treasure from America. I have felt from the beginning that the Libya campaign was doomed to failure.

It is the same old story repeated decade after decade with halfhearted efforts not capable of finishing successfully. Can you remember the American Air Campaign against the Serbs in Kosovo? The Serbs were systematically driving Muslims out of the country, killing many in the process. This should have been up to Europe to intervene if they felt compelled to do so. Instead President Clinton took on the responsibility using only air forces similar to the current campaign in Libya. Serbia was not a threat to European nations and certainly not to America. The point I am trying to make is that this was a regional conflict of a minor nature that Europe was incapable of resolving without the might of America. The concern about the USSR had diminished with the breakup on the Soviet Union. Russia while still powerful in and of itself had diminished as a concern. In actual fact around this time Russia had requested being included in NATO. The request was not approved.

The mighty coalition that had been NATO was now a shell of what it once had been. This would have been the time to re-evaluate the Alliance towards cooperation economically while reducing the American presence which even today is by far the largest contingent of NATO.

As I write this I understand that there are other nations ready to sign on to become members of NATO. There obviously is a need felt to join with others for the mutual good. Economic alliances are almost always beneficial. My concern is that the thought of overwhelming military force to combat Russia or some other major power does not exist without America.

We, as a country, are so deep in debt we are approaching a critical point where we won't be able to continue being the hero. Now would be a good time to re-evaluate, while the debate is raging in Washington concerning the deficit. They won't of course, as any retrenchment will be considered soft on defense. The horrendous cost of the current three wars plus maintaining bases throughout the world will continue. Our leaders will continue to muddle along until that fateful day not too many years from now when the rubber band snaps and fiscal reality sets in forcing drastic measures on Americans such as the people of Greece are now going through.

Jack B. Walters
June 30, 2011

Senator John McCain

What ever happened to the man I once supported to be President. He was a maverick then. During his last campaign to be re-elected as Senator of Arizona he proclaimed that he was never a maverick. I supported him when he ran against George W. Bush. When it looked like he was gaining support the Bush campaign put out scurrilous information that the black child in his family was sired by him.

During his later campaign for President against Obama he lost all credibility. He couldn't remember how many homes he owned. He cancelled a TV program with David Letterman to hurry back to Washington to save the Union, only to take the time to stop off for a more important interview with Katie Couric. The pictures of having his face powdered added to the hilarity of it. Then when he finally arrived, there he was sitting at the end of the table, not appearing to be making any important contribution. Who can forget his pronouncement that America's economy was in top shape just before the collapse leading to the TARP bailout of $700 Billion to rescue the largest financial institutions. I became really upset with him as he abandoned all pretense of representing Arizona in his position of Senator by campaigning continuously and with only a few exceptions did not cast any votes. I didn't think his little ditty "Bomb, Bomb, Bomb Iran", was very funny. Then he picked Sarah Palin as his running mate. A virtual unknown with little grasp of the national responsibility involved. This was the last straw for me.

All of the above issues are not why I decided to write this article. It is his continuing war mongering attitude toward any and all countries. He visited Libya and criticized Obama for not doing more. Then in today's headline picture, there he is in Afghanistan criticizing Obama for proposing bringing troops home at a faster pace than the Generals think prudent. If McCain was President he would pushing the military into more adventures than we are committed to at the present time. The Generals are probably right. To totally subdue the country we need more not less boots on the ground but if our goal (as I believe it should be) is to leave, then we should leave at a faster rate. No nation in history has been successful in dominating Afghanistan. I do not believe we can do it either. Here he is overseas while Congress has cancelled their July 4th break to stay in Washington to prevent our nation's defaulting on our debts; a far more serious dilemma than in 2008 when he "rushed" back. I can only conclude he has lost all semblance of what is important. If he can't bomb it, he just isn't interested.

Jack B. Walters
July 4, 2011

Republican Hypocrisy

If it wasn't so tragic it would be ridiculously humorous as we watch the antics of our newly elected members of the Republican Party as they battle President Obama over the necessity of raising the debt ceiling. All of a sudden the idea of raising it is abhorrent to them. Could it all just be an opportunity to embarrass the President and improve their chances with the voters in next year's elections?

Let's review the recent past;

Year	Debt Limit in Billions	Year	Debt Limit in Billions
1996	5,500	2007	9,815
1997-2001	5,950	2008	10,615
2002	6,400	2008	11,315
2003	7,384	2009	12,104
2004	7,384	2009	12,394
2005	8,184	2010	14,294

The reason the debt ceiling held steady during those earlier years was the result of the policies when President Clinton and the Democratic Congress were in power. Surpluses were being produced which were starting to lower the National Debt.

President Reagan and the first George Bush tripled the debt during their years in office. Under President George W. Bush together with his Republican Congress the debt ceiling was raised six times. Can anyone not remember Vice President Cheney's council to the President that President Reagan proved that deficits didn't matter? With that sage advice they went on their merry way. It was business as usual.

Immediately upon assuming office President Obama promoted his Trillion dollar stimulus plan. That together with the ongoing costs of the three "wars" we are engaged in has brought us to the brink. Now, all of a sudden the Republican House has said no more. I certainly agree the hemorrhage cannot continue. Where I disagree is that they are not seriously considering all options. In my opinion they have resolved to put the President in a box. In a separate article I will be spelling out areas that could be considered. All I hoped to accomplish with this one is to point out to those with short memories that the Republicans are like those living in glass houses. They should refrain from starting a rock throwing contest.

Jack B. Walters
July 6, 2011

President Obama and the Democratic Party's responsibility for the debt "crisis"

This is a follow-up of my last article entitled "Republican Hypocrisy". I promised I would have thoughts to share about the other group in this process.

President Obama was elected (in my opinion) out of frustration with President George Bush. There was never a President in my lifetime I felt who caused as much damage as he. The two unnecessary wars, no child left behind, senior drug program and general lack of leadership when it was so badly needed after 9/11. He pushed the country deep in debt in a haphazard fashion, totally without regard to the long term effect it would have on America. Jobs continued to leave America, going predominantly to China. With Americans losing good paying manufacturing jobs our tax base continued a downward spiral. He would not stand up to China, a country that uses every trick in their play book to suck jobs out of America. I won't take the time to enumerate as I have already done so many times in the past. He insisted on tax breaks for the wealthy and did nothing to lower the burden on manufacturing in America while enhancing large corporations to reap huge profits at the expense of American workers.

President Obama was given an overwhelming mandate including majority power both in the House and Senate. He could have provided a health care system similar to what most advanced nations enjoy. A program similar to Medicare extended for all our citizens. Instead he squandered many months trying to garner Republican votes, when any knowledgeable observer knew that wasn't going to happen. He started by accepting a huge handout from the drug companies as long as he didn't disturb their ability to charge Americans much higher costs than other nations by simply denying officials to use the huge market to lower costs. At the same time he allowed them to continue to advertise on television, the obnoxious ads we listen to night after night. Only one other country on earth allows this. Then he gave a gift to the insurance industry by mandating that all must purchase insurance. What I had hoped for was the elimination of the health insurance business. With them in control, nothing will keep from costs from escalating. Over 15,000 people are to be added to the government payroll to monitor citizens to assure they do sign up or pay fines or worse.

The Trillion dollar stimulus plan had virtually no effect on creating private jobs or for that matter public. It seems there weren't many projects ready to go. A huge part went to bail out State and local governments which while of benefit did not increase employment. Perhaps there were fewer layoffs but nothing positive. Unemployment benefits were extended and later on extended again. All of these people in their prime paid to stay home. As of 7/5/2011 the maximum period remains at 99 weeks. There were several hundred thousand persons who had run out of benefits. They were granted an additional 13 weeks but not over the 99 week maximum. There was nothing in the bill to enhance the private sector; no easing of regulations, no lowering of business taxes, no forcing China to allow their currency to float, no insistence on a level playing field. China provides many benefits to manufacturers who re-locate there, which makes it nearly impossible to compete.

President Obama expanded our forces in Afghanistan. While there are hopes that a steady withdrawal will occur, I am not holding my breath. At the same time it appears we are pleading with Iraqi officials to allow us to continue with 10,000 troops after the end of this year when all troops were slated to return. Then he authorized the bombing campaign against Khadafy in Libya in support of rebels who I believe will eventually be proven to be supporters of radical Islam. The fact is that even if justified we can no longer afford to play war games in this region. At some point we will pay the price here at home as those who hate us bring chaos to our shores.

All of my previous comments about Bush in relation to creating private sector jobs apply equally to President Obama. I need not repeat.

In an editorial today by Paul Krugman it seems corporations are once again lobbying for tax amnesty so they can bring their overseas profits back home without paying taxes. They received this break in 2004. They got it then. I have no doubt they will again which only further encourages moving jobs offshore.

My biggest concern with President Obama is what I perceive to be a lack of concern about the rising deficits. In fiscal year 2008/09 it was $1.885 Trillion. In fiscal year 2009/10 it was $1.652 Trillion. The projection this fiscal year is even higher and yet all he has proposed to date are matters that will have absolutely no effect on reducing the debt never mind curtailing deficits. He is, after all, the President, duly elected and charged with protecting Americans from enemies foreign and domestic. It is time for him to show strong leadership. This bickering between Parties must give way to tangible results. I could list a myriad of thoughts but what would be the use. Those elected officials should know and should get serious about doing the job they were sent to Washington to do.

Jack B. Walters
July 6, 2011

Another nail driven in the casket for American workers

For seventeen years Mexican trucks have not been allowed to enter America except to warehouses at the borders. The North American "Free" Trade Agreement had a provision to allow them access under specific guidelines. I want to state right at the beginning that in my opinion all of the so called free trade agreements were approved to the benefit of corporations not citizens of any of the three countries.

I have a question. Why was it our responsibility to spend $2.5 million to equip their trucks with monitoring devices? It would appear to me that Mexico should bear whatever costs are needed.

Mexico imposed tariffs on a dozen US made products in 2009. If we had leaders who cared about American workers we would have reciprocated at that time, tit for tat. But no, the so called super power once again allows the third world country to stomp on us; all the while we give Mexico billion dollar grants every year for assistance in their drug war.

The net effect will be to put pressure on American truck drivers to work for fewer dollars as the Mexicans will undoubtedly be paid far less. Each Mexican truck entering America will replace an American truck. This alone will have a devastating effect on American workers. Go ahead and say "they are only unskilled and don't deserve high pay". To you I say "walk in the other guy's shoes and see how you like it". One more sector of American workers being pressured to lower their life styles for the sake of consumers.

My last question is what ever happened to the members of Congress who had supported our truck drivers? Are they so busy trying to keep us from defaulting on the national debt that they dropped the ball?

Jack B. Walters
July 9, 2011

History of Libya

Out of my concern about the current military action by members of NATO on Libya, I decided to check out and learn about its history. I went to Wikipedia for my source. I didn't go back to the beginning of the world. I started in 1921 when Italy declared war on Libya and the Ottoman Empire (Turks) which at that time was in control of the coastal areas. The Treaty of Ouchey of 1923 included the withdrawal of all the Ottomans from Libya.

During WWI the Italians had to bring back their forces. During this period they lost control of all but the coast. In the 1920's under General Pietro Badoglio a bloody war was waged to pacify the natives. This continued until 1931 when the Arab leader was captured and hanged. The resistance then just petered out. Italy controlled Libya until 1943 when the North African Campaign conquered the country. Italy formally rescinded control in the Peace Treaty after WWII.

Beginning in 1945, anti-Jewish violence commenced. Many Jews were murdered; synagogues, homes and businesses were burned. When the State of Israel was recognized 30,972 Jews left for Israel between 1948 and 1951. By 1970 there were no Jews remaining.

In 1952 the United Nations granted independence. Oil was discovered in 1959. Exports began in 1963. Twenty eight year old Muammar al-Gaddafi staged a coup in 1969. He created a new Libya Arab Republic. The US vacated their last military base in 1970. In 1971 he nationalized the petroleum industry of British Petroleum. By 1972 he took control of all other petroleum companies up to 70%. He had to leave the rest as he needed their expertise to operate. He strongly supported the creation of OPEC in 1973.

His philosophy was neither communism nor capitalism. He created his own concept. He took ownership away from businesses and landowners who had more than they needed, in his opinion. On the positive side he did start two five year programs using oil revenue. The first was from 1976-80. The primary goal was to be food independent. The second from 1981-85 was to create industry. These were largely successful. He did increase the welfare of the people. By the 1980's they enjoyed improved housing, education, social services and general standards of health, the highest in North Africa.

He openly supported terrorism around the globe until 1986 when President Reagan bombed Libya bases and palaces. He stopped and as a result improved relations with the West by the early 2000's. In 2006 the US rescinded the designation of terrorist State. By 2007 Libya was elected to a non-permanent seat in the UN.

All of this brings us to this year. In Feb. 2011 anti-government rallies sprang up in Benghazi. On March 10, France recognized the National Council as the sole representative of Libya. Shortly thereafter a no fly zone was declared by NATO and air strikes began to punish Gaddafi's forces still loyal to him. Since then the air war has been expanded to striking military targets, Gaddafi's palaces or places he might be. It is obvious that his death is the goal. The coalition is breaking up. Italy has pulled out. Norway will end their participation August I, 2011. Gaddafi is still in power. The Army and much of the population still gives him their support, probably out of gratitude for what he has accomplished improving their lifestyles. In the review of recent history there was mention that he had cracked down hard on the hard core Muslims who require Sharia law as the only lawful government. Perhaps these are the ones who have broken away. In all the reporting to date their identity and objectives have not been revealed, at least not to my knowledge. What if the end result is plunging this country into chaos like the Taliban did in Afghanistan? The thought that these might be the people we are supporting is scary to me.

Rather than bomb Libya back to the Stone Age, if killing Gadhafi is the goal, then why not have another Seal operation. Kill him and then keep close watch on what happens next. Libya has suffered for 90 years starting in 1921 if you do not consider the ages prior to that date. Enough already.

Jack B. Walters
July 15, 2011

My grandson Chris's visit to Tucson
July 23-31, 2011

Sat 7/23/11

Roxanna drove us to Phoenix on Saturday to pick up Chris. We arrived with an hour to spare. His plane came in 10 minutes ahead of time but of course he was the last one off. When we left the terminal to the parking area he immediately commented on the heat. We found a Cracker Barrel restaurant as we were leaving Phoenix. Chris had French toast and bacon. He said it was great. Just as we entered the Tucson area Roxanna noticed a sign about Biosphere II. We hadn't planned it but decided since we were close to take it in. It was quite interesting. Chris really enjoyed it. We stopped for lunch at Bubb's Grub & Big Ten Saloon for a chicken barbeque lunch. Roxanna had heard about it. It was really very good. Then we stopped at the Conquistador Resort to see an international exhibit of tarantulas and scorpions. This was a hit for Chris. After moving in and unpacking, Roxanna made us sandwiches for a light dinner. I was going to take him swimming but he got hooked on a Harry Potter movie which we watched to the end, had ice cream and called it a day.

Sun 7/24/11

We decided to let him sleep in until about 8:30. Got him breakfast and went to church. Fortunately Judy Marvel was the guest minister. They mutually recognized each other. Chris met the congregation all of whom liked him. He was outgoing and friendly. He did recognize how small our congregation is. Today we numbered in the 20's. There was a spaghetti dinner afterwards, a fund raiser for a young girl to purchase school uniforms. From there we stopped at Target to buy Chris three pair of shorts, then on to Bookman's, a used book store, where he bought three comic books. After a short rest break he and I went downtown to see a King Tut exhibit. It consisted of replicas but was very good. He enjoyed it. We listened to a lecture for about 30 minutes until we were both ready to go home. Roxanna was going to take him swimming but the thunderstorm was approaching so she got him started sorting quarters by States. We have enough for two sets. If he gets it done he will bring one set home with him. After a delicious chicken noodle and corn dinner we settled in for 60 minutes after which I retired to start writing.

Mon 7/25/2011

It was a struggle but we were finally able to wake him up so we go meet our hiking club group at 5:30 AM for a two hour hike in Sabino Canyon. If you don't leave early in the summer you just can't hike at all. We introduced him to our friends but did not do the complete hike they were going on to Blackett Ridge. We returned home to eat breakfast then Chris and I drove to the Loft theatre where they are showing old children's movies from decades ago for free. It included free popcorn but poor Chris couldn't have because of his braces. We saw "The Seventh Voyage of Sinbad". We came home for lunch and then met another family for swim time at our association pool. He had a ball for three hours. At about the half-way point I left them in the care of Roxanna and the other adults to return home for a nap. It is tough to be old. In the evening we went to Pinnacle Peak restaurant in Old Dust Town which is located not far from here on Tanque Verde Drive. It is a quaint old west town with all kinds of interesting western buildings and stuff to see. During dinner we witnessed cutting men's ties. He got a kick out of it. It is an old custom done in jest to shame anyone coming in formal clothes. Then it was on to watch an old shoot em up show with lots of shooting, guys falling off roofs and dynamite blowing up. Chris really enjoyed it. We returned home for a light reading session before retiring.

Tues 7/26/2011

Chris had said he wanted to walk the dogs but when I tried to wake him at 6:30 he just wanted to sleep, so I let him until 8:00 AM. Roxanna had gone out early to climb a mountain called Little Elephant Head. After breakfast we again drove to the Loft theatre, this time to see "Swiss Family Robinson". Everyone really enjoyed it. We sat next to the family Chris had swum with the day before. The audience applauded when it was over. Afterwards he and I returned to Target to replace two pair of shorts, this time size 14. After lunch we again went to our community pool for swim time, three hours of constant activity with his new friends. A good meal courtesy of Roxanna and after calls home took it easy the rest of the evening.

Wed 7/27/2011

We woke him at 6:00 AM to meet with friends from the hiking club at 7:00. We just barely made it. This was special as we drove to Summerhaven near the top of Mt. Lemon to do a five mile, 1,100 ft elevation gain hike. At this elevation we hiked past Aspen groves and Ponderosa Pines in 70 degree temperatures. This was a relief to Chris and me from the desert floor heat. We were with about a dozen other hikers. They sang happy birthday to me during the trek. We rested in the afternoon, he doing it his way and me sound asleep. The hike really did me in. I hadn't done one like this for some time. That evening was our night at the Gas Light Theatre watching Gnat Man, a farce. Prior to that we had pizza at the diner attached to the show. As a result of Roxanna calling ahead I was recognized for my birthday and Chris for traveling from Alaska. We both received ice cream cones. The show was hilarious. Chris really got into the booing and hissing as did we all.

Thurs 7/28/2011

We got up at 6:30 today to get to the Desert Museum and enjoy it before the afternoon heat kicked in. There was cloud cover which moderated the heat. The highlight was a new program called "Running Wild" A number of live animals, birds and reptiles were brought out to be seen by the audience. Chris bought presents for Robin, Arden and Mom in the gift shop. Then it was haircut time at Debby's, just a trim, not a full cut that I had wanted. In the evening we went to a city bridge to watch the bats take flight about 7:20 PM. It was very enjoyable, then ice cream and to bed about 9:00 PM.

Fri 7/29/2011

5:00 AM today for golf at 6:30 AM. He did it. We joined Pat and Doug at Dorado Golf Course. Doug and I didn't play well but Pat did. Chris had fun feeding bread chunks to the ducks at the lake. Afterwards we had lunch together. He had a grilled ham and cheese sandwich with fries and lemonade. Then we stopped for groceries and cool time at home. After a dinner of pork chops prepared by me I took him to see "Transformers—the Dark Side of the Moon". It was nonstop violence. He said it was the best of all the rest. He finally explained on the ride home how to tell the good guys from the bad. The bad guys have red eyes and the cars are dull in color. We had ice cream bars and then to bed.

Sat 7/30 2011

This of course is my birthday. Surprisingly he woke up and came out at 6:00AM so after an orange juice we both walked the dogs, then I took him to breakfast at the Hungry Fox restaurant of French toast and bacon. The Reid Park Zoo was next. He enjoyed it as he had two years ago. It is well laid out with nice habitat for the animals. We came home to cool off and have lunch.

In the afternoon we visited the Miniature Time Museum. It is a collection of miniature buildings, furnishings, people, animals, etc, all of which are very well done. I can't say that it meant that much to Chris. We left after 45 minutes. After Roxanna returned from her hike and we had all cleaned up, we went out to celebrate my birthday at the Amber Restaurant. Bev. Larson joined us. The restaurant provided free desert, cheesecake and German chocolate cake. Then it was home to pre-pack and bed. Tomorrow we drive to Kathie Sharp's home in Apache Junction for lunch and then to the airport to send him home. I believe he enjoyed everything we tried to do for him in spite of the heat.

August 2, 2011—A date that will live in infamy

On this date the Congress finished their arduous work and President Obama signed the legislation adding an additional $2.2 Trillion to the National Debt limit. Conveniently it should keep us solvent until after the elections in 2012, so neither the President nor members of Congress will have to debate this subject during the election process. There is a pledge (worthless in my opinion) to find $2 Trillion in reductions over the next decade. A committee is to be established of 16 members of Congress equally divided between the Republicans and Democrats. It is to be created before the end of this year. No one it seems is anxious to volunteer to serve including our own fearless Senator Kyle. He stated in jest that his bladder could not stand the many hours of sitting to come up with ideas.

This is such an important subject that the exhausted members of Congress immediately adjourned until after Labor Day to recover from the ordeal. President Obama on the other hand immediately got on Air Force I for a campaign stop in Chicago. Regrettably he had to make a huge sacrifice by staying in Washington to deal with the "crisis". He missed ten fund raising events during that time. It is really a shame that he had to give up the activity he enjoys the most i.e. campaigning and raising money.

There was a time during my lifetime when governing was so important that full attention and total effort was expended to deal with the important issues of the day but no more. This is just a game for these people. They spend most of their time raising money for their re-election, always saying the right words that we want to hear but keep on playing the giveaway game to their benefactors. The Republicans favor the wealthy with tax breaks far in excess of what normal people pay and rewarding Corporations for sending our manufacturing and service jobs overseas. The Democrats keep giving money by any means possible to their base constituency to assure their loyalty at the ballot box.

There are so many obvious steps that could and should be taken right now, not a month from now. I won't bore you with my thoughts but trust me I have ideas. Instead of going on vacation they should be searching for immediate things to do to stop the hemorrhage. I will share one thought. Without increased tax revenue there is no hope of balancing the budget. The way I would do it is to eliminate the giveaway for sending jobs overseas and lower the cost of doing business in America. Millions of workers earning paychecks would start increasing the cash flow to the treasury without increasing rates. This is so obvious that my head hurts thinking about it. How does your head feel?

Jack B. Walters
August 4, 2011

Army Suicides—Arizona Daily Star-8/13/2011

I wonder if the hundreds of soldiers committing suicide has anything to do with the orders they must follow in these Arab countries of not responding until sure of the target for sake of offending the natives. They are trained for combat not house to house searches. The strain of wondering who is friend or foe and the ever present buried bombs plus the heavy load of weapons and protective gear they must carry has to be demoralizing.

My solution, bring them home, all of them.

Jack B. Walters
August 13, 2011

Solon Corp. cuts 60 manufacturing jobs in Tucson

Green energy was supposed to create jobs for Americans. This announcement from Solon shows it was all a charade. Our President is off campaigning in his fancy new bus while Congress takes a respite from their arduous efforts. I will tell you this would not happen on my watch. Assuming there will be a reduction in defense spending there will be other workers put on the street. We cannot continue the charade that we are a great country with all workers drawing unemployment benefits out of money we don't have.

Our taxation of business is the highest in the world. Is it any wonder manufacturers move to China to increase their profit? The only way to turn this around is to lower the cost of doing business in America. When Senator McCain suggested lowering from 35% to 25% the audience groaned. I seldom agree with him but in this case he was right. I don't know if 25% would reverse the outflow but certainly there are some intelligent people left in positions of power in Washington who could figure it out.

Am I upset with the management of Solon, you bet, but I am more upset with Obama and Congress for not creating a climate conducive for the growth of manufacturing jobs in America.

Jack B. Walters
August 16, 2011

Scoop of the Century

What is wrong with your editorial staff? On August 16, 2011, I wrote a letter to the editor entitled "Solon Corp. cuts 60 manufacturing jobs in Tucson". It was not deemed worthy to publish.

Day after day we read and listen to the President, members of Congress, candidates for President, the talk show hosts and columnists talking about jobs, jobs, and jobs. That word is the new buzzword being used to galvanize our people into voting for this or that candidate, or support one of the two major parties. Never or almost never do any of them talk specifics?

You search for all kinds of stories to put into print. The Solon decision should be assigned to your best investigative reporter, who then should drive out to the factory, take pictures, interview management and employees, contact top management which in this case is located in another country. Find out all the facts and then write a series of articles to shine light on what is happening all over the country. Soon, if nothing is done the only jobs left will be minimum wage jobs at McDonalds.

I spent my working life in manufacturing. It is a dog eats dog business. Every day you devote yourself and staff to find better ways of producing by lowering costs or increasing quality, or any of the many things needed to be competitive. In my day our community and our country were a part of that process. No more, only the bottom line.

Think about the process that resulted in the decision to take all the equipment off the floor, crate it, ship it and re-install thousands of miles away, then turn around and send the product back to Arizona for installation.

Think about the 60 employees who were making a reasonable wage, supporting their families, paying taxes, buying goods and services in our local economy. Now they will be added to the list of unemployed searching for jobs that no longer exist in America.

Vice President Biden is in China as I write this. I can assure you that nothing of importance will come out of his visit. I will also remind you that during the eight years of Bush the hemorrhage of jobs to China accelerated. China treats us like fools. They steal our jobs using every trick in the book including manipulating their currency to their advantage. All we do is ask for their kind indulgence. It is way past time to say enough and take tough, immediate action against China and the other countries taking our jobs and stand up for Americans and try to restore the American dream of a good life for our families.

How about it, won't you do your job?

Jack B. Walters
August 19, 2011

We have met the enemy and he is us

I try in vain to search for an issue, any issue that is supported by the majority of Americans. We continue to argue and fight among ourselves while the rest of the world continues to pass us by. My latest example is the report that was printed in today's Arizona Daily Star, from McClatchy Newspapers in regard to sit-ins in Washington against the construction of a pipeline which could deliver up to 1.3 million barrels of crude per day from our good neighbor to the North, Canada.

There are concerns about aquifers, crop land and property rights. I guess these protesters would rather continue getting oil from the Middle Eastern countries that use the gains to support terrorist organizations or build skyscrapers high into the atmosphere rather than promote the general welfare.

This has nothing to do with global warming. A barrel of oil is still only a barrel of oil no matter who provides it. Sometime hopefully we and the rest of the civilized world will wean us off of using oil but until that happy day, doesn't it make sense to get it from our neighbor.

While I am at it, we have proven reserves on the North Slope of Alaska equivalent to Saudi Arabia. We could be self-sufficient and bring our troops home from those god forsaken countries, fighting wars that cannot be won no matter how long we stay or how many more lives are lost.

These protestors are doing a disservice for our country.

Jack B. Walters
August 20, 2011

Private Sector Jobs

There can be no doubt that private sector jobs are disappearing in America at an accelerated pace. My main concern has to do with manufacturing but the service sector is also being diminished. When President Obama and Congress finally return from their vacations the ideas will be filling the newspapers and talk shows on a daily basis. Ideas usually proposed are; extend unemployment benefits, provide tax breaks for hiring employees, give billions to the States to assist them in resolving their respective shortfalls, continue under funding of Social Security by the 2% already in effect (further weakening the fund and shortening the time when funds will run out), infrastructure, etc. None of these will address the main point of creating private sector jobs. All of these will be a drain on our depleted treasury. Only private jobs will put money back into the treasury because the business and its employees will all be paying taxes. Not only that, but most manufacturing companies create other jobs in the community to support their mission. Taxes will accumulate from them as well.

It must be understood that business in order to be free must be allowed to pursue their endeavor as they see fit. They are duty bound to do all in their power to make a profit for their owners, whether stock holders or privately held. A company that is not successful goes out of business. It is as simple as that. If you do not believe in the free enterprise system then, of course, what I have just written does not make sense. Under Communism or Socialism, the government owns all property and makes the decisions on what should be produced. There are offshoots of these systems that have proven to be successful such as China which is a hybrid combining the power of the Communist State with allowing private enterprise to function on a small scale and subsidizing larger manufacturing who are competing with true free enterprise from America and elsewhere. There will come a time when this system will collapse. No country can continue to subsidize manufacturing. The problem for Americans is waiting for that to occur. In the meantime community after community in America loses more manufacturing jobs with nothing of value to replace the good paying jobs that have been lost.

Here is what I believe needs to be done. Evaluate all the reasons why manufacturing of products wanted in America are sent overseas. Certainly with all the high powered brains in Washington, this should be easy to accomplish. I want to be clear that I am talking about products to be sold in

America. Manufacturing goods for other countries use are better if located in the respective country for all kinds of good reasons.

So let's start. A study could be made of those companies that have moved their manufacturing or are in the process of doing so. I am sure the management would be willing to share the decision making process. Out of these interviews should produce a basis to start? High taxes are certainly a major reason. It is my understanding that America has the highest business tax rates in the world. Government restrictions and regulations are another. I read that some effort is being extended towards alleviating this burden while at the same time the clock is ticking on increasing regulations from the health care system approved two years ago. Certainly we need oversight of our food supply, drinking water and the air we breathe but I can tell you from my own personal experience that government regulations are a burden and detract from the primary mission of making a profit. China, in particular, does not burden their industry. Frivolous law suits are a continuing drain on profit. No large company would deliberately make unsafe products. Their goal is to entice repeat customers because of price, quality and service. Manufacturers are treated as if they were evil by intent. This is outrageous.

Skilled, industrious employees are a must. We are all aware that our educational system is failing our young people. Other countries are doing a superior job. If an employer cannot hire people capable of doing their assigned task then he must go to where he can find them. Right now China and India are leaving us far behind. I don't even know if trade unions exist today, those places where young people can learn to be electricians, plumbers, pipe fitters, welders, machine shop operators, and tool and die craftsmen. Thirty years ago we had them but as industry has faded away the need for these skills has diminished to where I doubt that a new startup company could hire these type individuals. I retired from what I like to refer to as a mature plant. What I meant by that, is that new people were being hired while at the same time older workers were retiring. We had all levels of skill working. We are losing the work ethic. Millions have been receiving financial assistance while not leaving there homes, whether welfare or unemployment. Each is as bad as the other. Once the work cycle has been broken there is generated a lack of interest in returning as long as the combined income for the family is sufficient to support the family.

The sum of what I am trying to say is that all factors being weighed by manufactures should be placed in the open and then formulate legislation that would mitigate the strength of these arguments. The recovery process might be long and perilous since factories already sent overseas would not readily return due to the high cost of relocating and the uncertainty of what the next Administration and Congress might do to reverse course once again as they have done repeatedly over the decades. An immediate result could be stopping the outflow so that more jobs are not lost. Over time, at least some factories would return those that are not labor intensive. After all it is extremely expensive to ship finished goods across the ocean. I know they have perfected shipping but regardless that is an expense. Then there is an increased assurance of higher quality products as a result of our stringent standards.

My last comment has to do with the weak kneed approach to China not only by the Obama Administration but during Bush's eight years in office. We continue to play the role of patsy allowing China to break every rule in the book from stealing our manufacturing secrets, to blackmailing manufacturers who do relocate to follow their edicts, to manipulating the value of their currency, to using child and prisoners in the work force, for lack of concern for safety and quality. Vice President Biden has just ended a "good will" visit to China. I can assure you that no pressure was brought to bear to keep more factories from closing and relocating to China. We hear words from time to time, particularly from those attempting to stay in office but regardless of fine words they just don't have the gumption to change the disastrous outflow of good paying jobs. It is up to us, the people to force them to do the job we send them to Washington to accomplish. I hope you will be one of those persons.

Jack B. Walters
August 27, 2011

It's not amnesty, and courts will be unburdened
Arizona Daily Star editorial—August 28, 2011

I would expect nothing less than your support for the program President Obama has put into place. He couldn't get Congress to approve his "Dream" Act so he accomplishes the same thing by executive order.

Of course the courts are jammed with cases and of course it makes sense to concentrate on criminals but have you ever asked the question of why? The process should be as simple as checking the person's ID. If not a citizen or legal immigrant that person should be escorted out of the country without delay regardless of when he or she entered this country. The current legislation should be amended to make the system work as it should.

It is a continuing mockery to build fences and hire border patrol agents when those who are able to slip through are now deemed acceptable to stay and now be granted work visas while others wait to enter legally. Of course 9% unemployment is of no concern as Americans are too lazy to take the jobs these people will do, or so you claim.

Jack B. Walters

So much for green jobs

In the news today was an announcement that Solyndra of Fremont, California declared bankruptcy and immediately laid off all 1,100 of their employees. This was the company that President Obama visited and touted as an example of his program creating "green" jobs. The US Energy Dept. provided a loan in March 2009 of $535 million to assist in getting started. Secretary Steven Chu promised the loan would create 4,000 jobs. Their product was solar panels. The President and CEO Brian Harrison stated "Regulatory and policy uncertainty in recent months created significant near term excess supply and price erosion".

On 8/15 Evergreen Solar Inc. and on 8/19 Spectra Watt Inc. filed bankruptcy. In Tucson just one week ago Solon Corp. laid off 60 production workers to send the jobs to China.

In China huge factories are being built or are already in existence to produce competing solar panels and other solar products. These are reported to be highly subsidized by the government.

The only comments I have heard from Republicans is to beat up on the President over granting the loan. When will they understand that private manufacturing jobs cannot compete when their competition is underwritten by a hostile government (China).

All the talk about creating jobs is hogwash. Is there no way to get Congress and the President to understand that jobs will continue to disappear all the while they debate.

Hello, hello, hello, are you up out of bed yet.

Jack B. Walters
August 31, 2011

Payroll tax cut idiocy

The beat goes on. Forget about future generations, they don't count. Just give us what we want now because we deserve it.

According to news reports, economists approve of reducing the payroll tax to 3.1% instead of 6.2%. The editorial you printed from the Kansas City Star urged support of it and the other proposals. The goal it seems is to put money into consumers' pockets so they can buy goods predominantly made in China. Continuing to provide unemployment checks year after year does nothing to provide American jobs. The other items in my opinion are gimmicks which require Federal employees to monitor to try to motivate employers to hire. My position has always been to create a climate to encourage growth letting the employer consider all the factors in deciding to produce here or elsewhere.

I have no doubt the Republicans will support the payroll tax cut with their "no tax increase" mentality. They have tried for decades to destroy Social Security. The Democrats are supposed to support it. It is well known that there are fewer workers putting money into the system as compared to those of us receiving monthly checks. I looked it up and found that should the funds continue feeding the Trust Fund before the last reduction, the Fund was projected to maintain itself for an additional 25 years. After that the outflow would exceed income by 25%. As of December 2010 there was $2.6 Trillion in the Fund. The Obama plan would decrease these funds by $175 Billion/year, not counting whatever loss might occur if companies increase their payroll by $50 Million. It has been stated that 50% of the population don't pay Federal Income tax therefore the only tax these people are aware of is Payroll. Shouldn't every person pay into a retirement system they will expect to benefit from?

I am fully aware that Congress for generations now has been using these Trust funds for general expenses meaning that the balance is not real money but IOU's from the government. Supposedly future government will make good. There is no guarantee which is why Governor Perry referred to it as a Ponzi scheme. He may be right.

Jack B. Walters
September 10, 2011

U.S. Senate votes tomorrow to force China to allow their currency (the YUAN) to float to its true value.

No wonder Americans are confused. Here is a clear cut issue that our government under Bush and now Obama has been unwilling to face head on. China's government does everything possible to add jobs for their people. This is admirable except for the extraordinary steps they have taken to achieve this goal. I will not fill this letter with them as it would take pages. This one issue, the YUAN, is on the table now, opposed vigorously by China, U.S. Corporations and Republican leadership, including Speaker John Boehner.

This one act would dramatically increase jobs for Americans and cost jobs for the Chinese. That is not our concern. The concern of Congress should be putting Americans back to work. Democratic Senator Harry Reid is pushing this bill. Wouldn't you think that the Republican leadership would join forces? Some Republicans are, as noted by the 79-19 advance legislation approved yesterday.

Jack B. Walters
October 5, 2011

Congratulations Mr. Cain

All news media are enthralled by the recent release of information that alleges sexual harassment, whatever that means. You should embrace it. Look at all the free publicity you are getting. Every show wants you to appear. You get your smiling face in front of millions. This would not be happening except for the fact that your message and unbelievable accomplishments to date have struck a chord in the hearts and minds of Americans of all political persuasions. Just think how great it would be to have a non-politician in the White House taking on the major problems of today without having had to grovel for funds from the moneyed interests.

Right now your attacks are no doubt coming from the Republican side. You are blowing away all of the other candidates. They will do everything to place doubt in the minds of Americans.

Hang in there. We need you.

Jack B. Walters
November 3, 2011

Why don't they get it?

First we were told that by the end of this year 5,000 troops would be leaving Iraq. I applauded the news, but now we are told that the new plans are to relocate 4,000 of them to Kuwait. No doubt they will be safer there than Iraq. The Pentagon officials and Defense Secretary Panetta have stated they expect to expand the U.S. military in the region to 40,000. The beat goes on. The American people have had a belly full of the useless expenditure of lives and funds trying to change century old traditions which are stubbornly adhered to. After 10 years you would think that someone in high authority would realize the futility of continuing and announce that our sacrificing has come to an end.

I have read in other articles that we spend one million dollars/year/ soldier. All the Super Committee has to do to fulfill their charge of reducing expenditures by $1.4 Trillion is to rapidly bring our troops home as quickly as they can consistent with an orderly withdrawal. I am not only thinking about the Middle East but worldwide. We are broke, not far behind Greece, but our leaders continue to act as if we had all the money in the world. We have carried water for Europe, the Middle and Far East for 60 years since WWII.

Using armies to conquer and control other nations has been archaic since the advent of the atomic bomb. Should Iran, N. Korea or other bandit nations start trouble we still have our long range missiles and aircraft that could inflict severe damage, enough so our opponent would cry uncle before very long.

Jack B. Walters
November 4, 2011

Herman Cain may quit his Presidential campaign

I can't wait any longer to put words to paper. It has been reported that tomorrow Mr. Cain will gather his supporters together, after talking privately with his wife, and announce the end of his campaign. This is all due to the harassment charges and lastly the accusation of marital infidelity with a woman he has known for 13 years and has aided financially. He has denied infidelity and denied the previous charges. Do I know, of course not, but here is what I do know. This man rose from poverty and strives to excel in every endeavor he ever attempts. He was very successful in achieving those goals. I bought and read his latest book. At the end are page after page of awards and recognitions he has received for achievement.

I do not believe a man like this could be guilty as he has been charged. Just for a moment let's say he is. For all of you who have worshiped at the feet of Bill Clinton, I wonder if this woman did to Cain what Monica did for Clinton. How soon we forget.

Mr. Cain had captured the imagination of Republicans and had surged ahead of the pack. They and people like me were excited to think of a non-politician leading our country out of the morass we are in today. I can remember the debate where all of the other candidates jumped on him over his 9/9/9 proposal. Then all hell broke loose with the accusations. To me this was an orchestrated, successful attempt to get rid of him. The fact that Republicans were rooting for him put the lie to racism. The talk show hosts for the most part have ridiculed him. Certainly the late night hosts have had a field day.

If he caves tomorrow, we will have lost a great opportunity and will be left to choose among whoever is left standing. Any thinking, caring person must choose an alternative to our current President.

Jack B. Walters
December 3, 2011

P.S. On December 4, 2011 he did as predicted and quit his campaign.

Your editorial today, "Dems, GOP need to
come together on payroll tax cut".

I disagree. Continuing to not fund the Social Security Trust Fund only hastens the day when the well runs dry. If only funding part of it is OK, then why not go all the way and stop funding it at all? No responsibility for the future, just please the electorate short term.

As to unemployment extension, quit doing it piecemeal, one extension after the other. If the intent is to provide income for not working and contributing to the general welfare then just extend it forever.

I am from the generation that was willing to sacrifice for the good of the country. The "me" generation rejects that concept and demands give a ways. They have somehow concluded they deserve it. Since they get their way, I guess they are right.

Jack B. Walters
December 4

Revenge of the Electric Car
(A Documentary Film)

I and six others were in the theatre this evening to see this outstanding presentation of the trials and tribulations of the process of bringing electric cars onto the market. It starts with the well documented destruction in 2006 by General Motors. There were several hundred on the road in California. The lessees really liked the car. Since they were not allowed to purchase, they could not prevent G.M. from taking them back and crushing them to be sure they could not be put back into service. This film follows one that chronicled the saga. It was called "Who killed the Electric Car". I wrote an article after seeing it. To this day it is hard for me to forgive G.M. management. That is why I was outspoken against the Federal Government bailout.

This new film covers the years since 2006. There is a small company that is retrofitting gasoline cars with batteries. It is a mom and pop type of enterprise run by Greg Abbot. Their main contribution is to provide an alternate as opposed to a newly designed electric car. Carlos Chosn of Nissan is by far the most aggressive. He is staking their future on the success of the Leif and other electric cars. Bob Lutz was instrumental in convincing G.M. management to develop the Volt. Elon Musk started his own company called Tesla Motors in California. He almost went under but is today in production with great looking cars.

We are all aware of the hybrids produced by Honda and Toyota. At the end there are brief glimpses of autos from Europe and also trucks on the road today. How great it would be if electric cars became a larger part of the vehicles on the road, particularly in places like California with the smog produced by gasoline vehicles. You don't even have to believe in global warming to see the advantage. Wouldn't it be great to stop sending billions to the countries in the Middle East most of whom hate us.

As I usually do I will end this with a plea to our elected officials and the American consumer. This progress can be brought to a screeching halt if gasoline prices continue to drop. The higher cost and limited range will keep consumers from purchasing as the gas savings will not be sufficient, even though we would all appreciate cleaner air to breathe.

I highly recommend seeing this film.

Jack B. Walters
December 14, 2011

2012

2012

Listing in order by date

1- Muslim Threat to World Peace

2- Calling all Independents to action-January 11

3- Kunde is gone-January 25

4- Response to Jim Driscoll's letter praising Obama's decision on the pipeline January 25

5- Catholic Church controversy over being required to provide birth control insurance for employees-February 14

6- Insanity in Afghanistan-February 27

7- Its Income Tax Time Again-March 1

8- Something's wrong here-March 8

9- And so it continues-April 18

10- Corporate Offices-Universal Studios letter-April 14

11- Same Sex Marriage-May 10

12- Screwed-a book report-May 17

13- A Chink in the Armor-May 26

14- Metal Thefts in Tucson-May 28

15- Ellen Donohoe letter-May 29

16- Short discourse on the evolution of Social Security-June 2

17- Special Election-June 13

18- Dark Clouds gather over the land-June 29

19- The Post-American World-a book report-July 5

20- Seven Killed in Afghanistan-July 10

21- Deception of our elected officials-July 13

22- Rep. Bachman's new McCarthyism deserves censure-July 21

23- Offshoring and Repatriating U.S. Jobs-July 22

24- 2016:Obama's America-a documentary film-September 1

25- Who is the Racist?-September 10

26- The Party is Over-a book report-September13

Muslim Threat to World Peace

Americans are living in ignorance about the onslaught of the Islamic juggernaut that has infiltrated every country on earth. Their declared goal as expressed by the deceased Gadhafi is to transform all countries to Islam and further that it can be accomplished by immigration and uncontrolled birth rates. Most civilized nations including our own offer subsidies for immigrants to get settled including housing. They choose to accept but do not become a part of society as other groups have in the past. They tend to keep together operating under Sharia law while ignoring the laws of their new country. Females, in particular, are kept from meeting and dating men who are not Muslim. In strictly Muslim countries activities such as above would justify honor killing of daughters. A Muslim woman raped must find four or more male witnesses to support her claim. Muslim men can marry girls as young as nine years old.

Don't take my word for it, just read articles any day in the Arizona Daily Star. Just today on page A19, Sri Lanka Muslims are demanding that tourist resorts be shut down because liquor is available, that direct flights from Israel and steps to end flogging of females found to have sex outside of marriage be stopped. On page A17 there was a picture of a fifteen year old girl in Afghanistan, tortured and confined to a cellar for refusing to be a prostitute. The article was positive in that the story was even allowed to be made public. I disagree and condemn the barbaric practices continuing in effect around the world. I agree with author Donie Darwish that Islam is not a religion. It is a way of life dictated by Sharia law and is similar to Communism and Nazism in that they are evil systems.

You should be aware of the love affair our current President has with Islam. If not, just Google "Obama's Cairo Speech". This was given early in his presidency. I have yet to hear any Republican candidate for President even mention the subject as a concern. Only informed citizens will bring this out into the open where, who knows, perhaps they can become part of the progressive world. If not, then the world as we know it will end, and not too far into the future either.

Jack B. Walters
January 5, 2012

Calling all Independents to Action

I believe that voters who have registered as an Independent did so as I did to show that we have lost faith in the two major parties. We long for the day when we can have our own candidate not tainted with Corporate or Union dollars but today is not the day.

In February the Republican Party will hold their primary. Only registered Republicans can vote. Since I am unequivocal about the need to remove Obama from that office I picked up a registration form today and have re-registered as Republican. After the primary I will re-register as Independent.

I am requesting other Independents to emulate my example. You have until the end of January to send in. Forms are available at Post Offices and Libraries. Who you want to support is of course your decision but to let this opportunity pass by was not acceptable to me.

Jack B. Walters
January 11, 2012

Kunde is Gone
January 25, 2012

We put Kunde down this morning. He was the kindest gentlest dog I ever owned. He was special to Roxanna as well. He loved everyone and everything. He would wag his tail any time he met people or other animals.

One year ago in February we took him to the vet as he was having problems breathing. It had gotten progressively worse until he couldn't lie down and rest because then he couldn't breathe. We thought then we would have to put him down but Dr. Matz gave him medication which relieved the liquid buildup around his heart and prescribed daily pills to keep the liquid from building up again. He was frank with us and advised Kunde might only live a few more months or at the most one year. He almost made it.

About four days ago he started acting differently. He didn't want to eat and had a rough cough. Roxanna mixed rice in with his food and he ate sparingly. Last night after I went to bed he woke me up as he sometimes does. I let him out to piddle only to find that he had already done so in the hall and family room. Later he woke Roxanna up and kept her up the rest of the night letting him in and out and worrying because he was so tired but could not lie down and rest. We contacted Dr. Matz as soon as he arrived at the clinic. He told us to bring him in right away. After a quick examination he told us it was time. There was nothing more he could do. He suspected kidney failure on top of the fluid buildup. He prepared him for the injection while we waited in a comfortable room overlooking a garden. He brought him in for us to have our time with him. Roxanna let him walk around the garden then we called for the Dr. There was no sign of trauma. He just slowly stopped breathing.

Last year Roxanna lost her beloved Cisca and now Kunde. We still have Boomer and Chica to care for. Whenever their time comes that is it for us. No more pets. Pets have always been an important part of our lives but at our stage of life neither of us wants to start over again with all owning pets entails.

We are having him cremated. It is our intention to take most of his ashes back to Kunde Mountain where this all began September 15, 2001, just four days after 9/11. Hiking friends have stated they would join us as we commemorate his life. We will place a few next to Cisca in our back yard.

It's Income Tax Time Again

I spent most of yesterday filling in my Federal and State Income Tax forms. Mine are fairly simple but even so I have a number of calculations to compute along the way. What really boggles my mind are the myriad of deduction lines and their accompanying forms none of which mean anything to me.

It is obvious that over the centuries legislatures have provided these to aid any number of causes. I will give them credit for their efforts but what a nightmare has been created. I'll bet some of these items are not even relevant today but you can bet someone is taking advantage.

A taskforce should be put together with the aim of simplification and fairness. Fraud could be reduced if not eliminated. The staffing of the Revenue Departments could be reduced or put to better use catching the really big tax cheats. You know the types that use the Cayman Island to hide their gains.

When I lived in Canada 40 years ago I was amazed at the simplification of their forms. There was one form for both the Federal and the Provinces. It was a one page with lines on both sides. I don't remember exactly but there was a deduction for me, my wife and children, a standard deduction and additional for medical. This was before they nationalized health care so that probably doesn't exist today. The interesting thing was that after you determined your total tax, all that was required for the Province was to multiply it by a percentage. That was the amount that would be returned to the Province. No additional State forms as we must fill out. Can you imagine the cost to pay for staff to review our forms as they are submitted?

Jack B. Walters
March 1, 2012

Response to Jim Driscoll's letter praising Obama's decision on the pipeline.

I disagree with Mr. Driscoll. Obama was wrong. The environmentalists that protested the pipeline were wrong. The pipeline has nothing to do with global warming. The issue is the chance to receive energy from our neighbor to the North instead of Saudi Arabia and the rest of OPEC. Any time we can reduce the flow of billions annually to them we decrease their ability to cause harm for the civilized countries. The Muslim onslaught has got to be stopped. One good way would be to dry up their petro dollars. The other best way would be to remove all barriers to oil and gas production in the United States.

Sure, we all agree solar, etc. would be preferred but until that day we must protect ourselves and the best way is to return to those days when we did export energy to the world. We stopped to take advantage of cheap Arabian oil. Then it was $4.00/barrel. Now it is $100/barrel.

Jack B. Walters
January 25, 2012

Catholic Church controversy over being required to provide birth control insurance for employees

I have a few points to make. In the first place what gives the Federal government the right to insist that a company provide health insurance for its employees? In my day issues like this were the subjects discussed at the bargaining table for those companies with unions. For those without unions, in order to be competitive in the labor market companies provided benefits. Now all of a sudden the Federal government is dictating. Does anyone besides me believe it is none of their business?

The controversy has been swirling around for the past week or so. On a drive back to Tucson from Phoenix yesterday, for entertainment benefit, I listened to Rush and Sean. They repeatedly bashed Obama for interfering with religious beliefs and forcing religions to go against their tenants. While it is always good policy to criticize Obama it is my belief that Obama is using this issue to pave the way for something far more important to him. That is allowing Muslims to live under Sharia law as dictated by the Koran. This has been successful in England and other countries. It has been tried in our country. In fact at least one State tried to get ahead of the curve and outlaw it. As I recall it was struck down by the courts.

My point being that the right wing talk show hosts are digging a grave by demanding that the government not interfere with religious beliefs. They will not be able to talk differently when Sharia becomes the topic.

I believe Obama is a disaster for America. I do not believe he is ignorant or uninformed. He knows exactly what he is doing and why. Remember you heard it first from me.

Jack Walters
February 14, 2012

Insanity in Afghanistan

Copies of Qurans may have been burned by our military. The entire country is in an uproar and a number of Americans have been murdered. This continues the farce we witnessed in Denmark several years ago over a cartoon. Any perceived insult to Islam is a free license to kill at random.

Obama, McCain, Romney and others proclaim the need to continue the mission that has dragged on already for over a decade. It is insanity to continue. If we stay 20 years or longer nothing will change. There is concern about the return of the Taliban and al-Qaida. They will return regardless. We only delay the inevitable. We should have destroyed their training camps rather than occupying the country. Many American lives lost and trillions squandered.

I cast my vote for Ron Paul. He has the courage and wisdom to end this farce.

Jack B. Walters
February 27, 2012

Something's wrong here

Do you ever wonder about decisions made on our behalf in establishing relationships with leaders around the world? I will confine my remarks to the Middle East although it could easily be expanded to include South and Central America where for decades we have supported Dictators who oppress their own people.

I loved the picture of Don Rumsfeld shaking hands with Saddam Hussein when Iraq was at war with Iran. We gave him Billions in aid including poison gas he used not only against Iran but also Iraqi Kurds in the North where thousands were killed.

After Gadhafi capitulated on weapons of mass destruction he was welcomed into the United Nations with our support.

We went to war with the Taliban and al Qaida in Afghanistan ostensibly to punish them for the 9/11 terror attack based on the assumption that the terrorists received their training there. I always thought that was a mistake since 16 of the 19 involved were from Saudi Arabia.

Under the rule of the Taliban, women were removed from the work force, girls from schools and they were forced to stay in their home and only be allowed out with a male escort wearing burkas that covered them from head to toe.

When the Taliban were defeated we supported Hamid Karzai in becoming President. Now I read in the Star on 3/7/2012 that in order to help persuade the Taliban to live in peace he has instituted the same shameful rules which amounts to subjugation of all women in that country. This is the same man our President apologized to recently over the burning of Quran books. I never read that Karzai apologized for murdering our soldiers indiscriminately in retaliation for that act.

I guess our strategic interests are more important than promoting freedom and justice for members of the female sex. Not in my book. After spending a trillion dollars and the loss of thousands of lives this is what we have to accept for our effort. I say shame on all our elected and military leaders. There was a time when they valued human rights issues.

Jack B. Walters
March 8, 2012

And so it continues

In today's Daily Star (4/18/2012) is another article relating to Afghanistan. It consists of demands from Afghan President Hamid Karzai that the United States pledges a minimum of $2 billion /year to support their military after we leave in 2014. U.S. officials were quoted as expecting to provide $4 billion. The amount is expected to be finalized at a conference to be held in Chicago in May. What Karzai wants is a firm commitment not just some vague promise.

Our country is operating with an annual deficit of $1.2 trillion. Keep that thought in your head as you ponder the wisdom of an open ended commitment of this amount for decades to come. How insane is this.

At least when Russia called it quits after they lost they took what remained of their marbles and went home. Their defeat among other things ended up breaking up the USSR as they were nearly bankrupt. In my opinion we are nearing that same situation. How can a responsible government continue to give vast sums away that we borrow from China?

One last thought, I wonder how much we are continuing to give to Iraq after pulling out our forces. I have never read anything but I would venture to guess it is similar to what Karzai is demanding.

I have written many times about bringing our troops home, now I am asking to keep our money home as well.

Jack B. Walters
April 18, 2012

Corporate Offices   April 14, 2012
Universal Studios Plaza
Orlando, Florida
32819-7610

Dear Sirs,

On April 4, 2012, I accompanied my son and his family to spend the day at your Universal Studios Theme Park. They were interested in checking out the new Harry Potter attraction. I live in Arizona, my son lives in North Carolina. His family and I came to Florida to spend time with my daughter-in-law's mother who lives in Plant City. As an 83 year old senior citizen I had no particular interest other than spending time with my family regardless of what they might want to do.

We got up early and arrived just as the Park was opening. Even so there was already a long line to enter. We accepted this. We headed directly to the Harry Potter area and got to the end of the line not realizing that we would stand in the slow moving line for over one and one half hours after which we were allowed to take the four minute ride. We were a little tired and hungry so we stopped and bought lunch, then we proceeded to the Spiderman area and once again got in line. This time nearly two hours passed before we were allowed to take that three minute ride. As we neared the end I observed the man who was directing traffic. My estimate is that he allowed four of the VIP persons to one from the long line. They probably waited 10 to 15 minutes. No regard or consideration for the rest of us. I kept my piece as I didn't want to offend my son but I was outraged at this total disregard for the well-being of the thousands of guests such as us, many of whom had small children and others old like I am. My son advised me he spent $85 per ticket.

My recommendation would be to eliminate the VIP program as it is at the present time where, as I understand it, anyone can receive that status for an additional $25. Reserve VIP for VIP's such as elected officials, celebrities, etc. To recover the lost funds increase the daily admission charge. If patrons were standing in a line that was continually advancing there would be far fewer disgruntled customers.

Obviously you are making a huge profit. The amount of funds to create these magnificent structures and rides must have been enormous. The staff training and the huge number required must also be a huge expense. If at the end of the day you have thousands with unhappy experiences such as we had then what have you accomplished other than adding up the proceeds. Not that it makes any difference from my home in Tucson but I will never recommend anyone to visit Universal Studios in Orlando.

Yours truly,
Jack B. Walters

Same sex marriage

I decided to go on record with my opposition to this issue. As of yesterday President Obama declared he is in favor of it. This followed Vice President Biden's declaration a few days ago. The timing is incredible since North Carolina had just overwhelmingly approved a Constitutional Amendment to state that marriage is between a man and a woman. It was already a State law but they felt seriously enough about it to lock it in stone. Already Democrats are demanding that their convention site be moved out of Charlotte. I will follow this with amusement. The only thing positive about Obama's statement is that he recognizes that this is a State issue. Most States have taken positions similar to N. C.

While I have accepted civil unions since there appears to be many people in this country that prefer companionship with others of their same sex, I will not change my opposition to marriage. Show me somewhere, anywhere in a religious text where this was deemed acceptable. You can't, because it is not there. I am a live and let live type of guy. If that is how they want to live I could care less, but to taint the sacredness of marriage is intolerable to me. The first time I hear that a marriage of this type is going to happen at a church I am supporting that will be my last day attending. As tolerant as I have tried to be in my life, this is the point of no return for me.

I just thought you should know.

Jack B. Walters
May 10, 2012

Screwed
By Dick Morris & Eileen McGann

I caught an interview on talk radio where Dick Morris was discussing his just released book "Screwed". Upon returning home I placed an order for it. I have not been disappointed. I have known about him for many years beginning when he was the political advisor to Bill Clinton. I have always held him at arm's length since he appeared to me to be a turncoat moving from one party to the other or in the news media, able to sell whatever he was promoting at the time.

The reason I jumped at buying his book is that much of what was purported to be in it were ideas I have firmly held for decades. I was not disappointed, nor will you if you also read.

Many of you know that my own personal writing is often blunt. I purposely present my thoughts without ambiguity. Other writers try to be balanced. I see no need to follow their example. There are more on the other side so I feel free to state my case in a simple direct fashion.

There are eleven chapters, each devoted to a specific area where we Americans are getting the short end of the stick. They are;

1- A World Without Democracy; America Without Sovereignty
2- Trick or Treaties; How the European Union is Preempting Congress and Binding Us Through International Treaties
3- China
4- Pakistan
5- Afghanistan
6- Saudi Arabia
7- The United Nations of Corruption
8- The World Bank
9- Foreign Aid; Biting the Hand That Feeds Them
   In Our Backyard; The Chavez-Ahmadinejad Alliance
10- The Enemy Within

I listed the chapters to give you an idea of the subject matter. I am not going to try to give a summary of each as it would need to be voluminous. I will state without exception that I support his ideas in total. As I stated at the beginning most of these thoughts I have written about since I began in 2003. Let me just say that any or all of these problems could be resolved if we could ever have a President and Congress who put the interests of America ahead of foreign countries and greed. The obscene money being earned by former elected officials is revolting. They sign on as lobbyists and promote the interests of foreign regimes against the best interest of America, often supporting issues which as a Congress person they previously opposed. He names people who I am sure you will be shocked to learn about from both parties. Money it seems is all that is important.

We are constantly being deceived into voting for or against a person. We give outlandish amounts of money in the vain hope that when elected they will steer a straight course not allowing lobbyists to consume their personal time or accept their financial support. We are losing big time.

My book is available for anyone to read. I hope at least some of you will obtain the book and after reading try to galvanize others to get involved.

Jack B. Walters
May 17, 2012

A Chink in the Armor

Following the NATO Summit in Chicago last week, the newly elected French President Hollande advised President Karzai that effective the end of this year all French combat troops would leave Afghanistan. He would leave a few to orderly remove military equipment and trainers. This created consternation with the other NATO members.

I welcome this break in unity of this cold war inanity. NATO has long ago ended its usefulness. The air war against Libya was mostly an American effort. Russia has long ago ceased being a threat to Europe.

Continuing armed forces in Afghanistan only prolongs the inevitable. No matter how much treasure and blood we commit to it nothing will ever change for the better. They must decide on their own what kind of country they want to be.

It is my fervent hope that other nations follow the example of France and the coalition dissolves in the process.

Jack B. Walters
May 26, 2012

Metal Thefts in Tucson

Darren DaRonco,

This note is in response to your article in the Arizona Daily Star 5/27/2012. It is astonishing to me the helplessness of law enforcement to solve any problem whether it is bank robberies, graffiti, drugs or metal thefts. All should be easily solved.

As to metal theft, I have the following thoughts to share;

If legislation is required then law enforcement should petition for change. If that is not the case then all places where scrap metal is purchased should be required to obtain the "real" address and name of the person selling. They should be required to state where the metal was obtained. Having staff review this information it should soon be easy to find who are routinely selling. If they are not legitimate contractors then their residences should be inspected. Perhaps surveillance could be used in the evenings to watch for traffic and tail the suspects.

They devoted countless hours searching for the missing girl. That is, of course, important but so is theft on such a massive scale, $600,000 since January as stated in your report.

Once found then throw the book at the perpetrators to send a clear message.

I hope you will share these thoughts with the appropriate city officials.

Yours Truly,
Jack B. Walters

Ellen F. Donohoe   May 29, 2012
Executive Director of the Founders Campaign
Hillsdale College

Dear Ellen,

You are not going to enjoy reading this letter. I am quite disturbed and want
to tell you why. On your visit to Tucson we met at Mimi's for coffee. I arrived
before you did and watched as you collected an armful of literature to give to
me. Included was Dr. Folsom's latest anti FDR book entitled "FDR goes to
war". You should be aware by now that I am not a fan of Dr. Folsom. I have
read his books including this last one out of respect for you. I believe I shared
my book reports with you.

Later at the conference held at Starr Pass I noted on the free tables all of
the literature that you had given me previously including stacks of his latest
book. I took it all in stride and shortly thereafter mailed in my contribution of
$1,000, the same amount I had given previously. I enjoyed the conference and
came away feeling I had learned from it.

I am a prolific reader of serious material and have books by my chair on
a continuous basis. After finishing my latest "Franklin and Winston" I found
I had finished all in the house. Your stack of literature had been placed next
to my chair unread. Yesterday I picked it up and started reading. All was fine
until I came across Dr. Folsom's article from the American Spectator entitled
"FDR's Class Warfare: A Tutorial For Obama". I am deeply offended.

To me this was the straw that broke the camel's back. To compare FRD
with Obama is a sacrilege to me. They are light years apart. FDR was my
American hero. Obama is a man of low character who cares nothing for
America or Americans. Every program he has pushed since becoming President
I have opposed. Every day he remains in office our country deteriorates a
little more. For the record I had no respect for George Bush either. I made
the mistake of voting for both of them mainly because I couldn't accept the
opposing candidates. I did not vote for Bush the second time around nor
will I vote for Obama this November. I am not particularly enamored with
Romney but I have no choice.

I gave you free copies of the books I had written. Perhaps you or others read
some of the articles. To complete this letter I am attaching three from my books
for a refresher and my latest Franklin and Winston book. If you read them they
will explain my reasons for listing FDR as second only to Lincoln in greatness.

I have believed in the Hillsdale philosophy which is why I started to provide financial support. The thought of Dr. Folsom poisoning the young minds of your special students is atrocious to me. I feel the same way about those attending your seminars. Are they coming away with negative thoughts about FDR too? I will not take any more of your time batting this subject back and forth. I am not a person who can be placed in a category like Tea Party, etc. I believe today's corporate leaders have abandoned Americans searching for the highest profit without regard to the loss of good paying manufacturing jobs as were available in my day. G.M. boasts that 70% of manufacturing is overseas. They are building research centers in China. G.E. has done the same with their X-ray production and research for example. I consider these treasonous acts which our government seems powerless to affect, both parties. It is all greed. I am sick of it all.

I am requesting that you advise President Arnn and Dr. Folsom of my feelings on this matter. I realize my small contribution is of little importance but I will not be continuing in the coming years if this assault on the character and leadership of FDR continues.

Sincerely yours,
Jack B. Walters

Short discourse on the evolution of Social Security

Social Security was enacted in 1935. Taxes started being collected in 1937 and the first benefits were provided. In the early years the beneficiaries were granted income far in excess of their own personal contributions. That was to be expected and should not have been a concern. It had to start sometime and the vestiges of the great depression were still being felt. The payments, even as low as they were, aided poor people who were desperate.

At first only men were eligible. As the years passed by, the Act was amended many times to include house employees, farm labor, etc. The amount deducted and the benefits paid were also adjusted nearly on a two year cycle. This continued until 1956 when Dwight Eisenhower was President. At that time SSDI (Social Security Disability Insurance) was added. This provided benefits to disabled persons below the age of 65. Eisenhower opposed it but did sign into law after passage by Congress. It was funded by the Social Security Payroll Tax. Disability can be mental, back pain and other hard to prove ailments. Wikipedia reports that in 2002, 7.2 million people were receiving benefits. This increased to 10.6 million in 2011.

In 1972 when Richard Nixon was President SSI (Supplemental Security Income) was approved. This program provides income for people over 65 and blind or disabled children. It is funded by General Revenues. At the same time, people in the SSDI program were made eligible for Medicare after receiving benefits for 24 months.

It is my contention that the SSDI program enactment and subsequent amendments paid for with funds from the Social Security Trust Fund has drastically depleted funds from its original intention, thereby hastening the doom for the Fund. The monies placed into it to provide supplemental income for seniors is now being siphoned off at an ever increasing amount to where today it is rapidly depleting the Fund. This never should have been allowed to pass. It is not that I am insensitive to those in need; it is that welfare should be handled separate from old age insurance and Medicare.

The reason I am taking the time to write this paper is after receiving an e-mail yesterday entitled "Where are the gray hairs". It showed a picture of a Social Security Office filled to overflowing with obviously much younger people applying for benefits.

Another interesting piece of information I gleamed from my research was that in 1983 when Reagan was President, Social Security income was taxed for "rich" people; singles earning $25,000 and families $32,000. Every year when I prepare my income tax, I am angered that I must do the calculation to see how much of it will be taxable income. The funds taken out of my paychecks during my working years amounted to fewer funds available to support my family. The only justification could be to add funding to run the government.

It is a wonder to me that anyone bothers to work today. There are multiple ways to scam the system; the items mentioned above, food stamps, unemployment compensation extended year after year, free health care for those deemed in need, welfare checks, income to support arts and studies of all kinds. Just look at your income tax form to see the many lines that can be used to decrease taxes paid. I read recently that many holders of food stamp debit cards sell them to others and claim they were lost. This can happen multiple times without recourse, unbelievable to me that safe guards cannot be enacted to correct abuses like this.

I see little hope for sanity to somehow be discovered. The truth is no politician (either party) has the gumption to correct issues like the above, since they must pander for votes. How far have we fallen when the citizens must be bribed for their votes? Whatever happened to patriotism, self-reliance and responsibility?

Farewell to the American dream of a free country better than all the rest, full of movers and achievers. A major reason has been our government's inability to preserve good paying manufacturing jobs. Our companies pay the highest corporate taxes of any other country, our regulations are far more restrictive and costly, we allow countries like China to manipulate their currency and steal our industrial secrets, all for the sake of Wal-Mart shoppers searching for the lowest cost merchandise.

Jack B. Walters
June 2, 2012

Special Election

It's over now. Barber will hold the seat at least until the end of the year. Up to now I have held my tongue but now want to say the whole charade was a farce. Everyone of course felt empathy for Giffords. Our district had muddled along for over a year without her operating as an able bodied member of Congress. As I understand it the election cost the taxpayers over one million and there were at least 2.2 million spent in political advertising. What a waste of resources and the time taken by many during the process. I can only assume the Democratic leadership felt it would be to their advantage to do this to assure re-election in November.

Jack B. Walters
June 13, 2012

Dark Clouds Gather over the Land

This has been an historic week for the Supreme Court and America.

They ruled in favor of the health care law by naming the cost to not purchase health care a tax. They ruled that in protecting free speech it is permissible to claim military service and medals earned. They threw out most of SB 1070. The one part they allowed was abrogated immediately by Obama ordering Homeland Security to not co-operate with Arizona law enforcement, making it a hollow victory.

What this means to me is that States Rights have been compromised. My reading of the Constitution is that the intent was to give maximum power to the States with only a few well defined rights to the Federal Government. With the new power to tax whatever they want the Federal Government will reign supreme. These are not political issues, they are States Rights Issues.

Jack B. Walters
June 29, 2012

The Post—American World
By: Fareed Zakaria

A liberal leaning friend shared his copy of this book with me. As I have always tried to do I read it to see what I could glean from it of value in my continuing search for reason and solutions?

I believe it to be a valuable source of information and I share his views on where America stands today as all around us other nations are gaining ground. He believes as I do that we are still dominant and will continue for some time in the future.

He does point out many ways in which we have hurt ourselves most importantly the bombastic way in which President George Bush went to war with Iraq without a mandate from the United Nations which meant that for the most part we went alone. The first Iraq war we not only had military support from our traditional Allies but also the Arab League. Unbelievable to have them fighting side by side with America. In addition many billions were given to defray the cost. The second time around America did the fighting and paying. The vast majority of citizens around the world including myself expressed their concern to their governments hoping to stop it. Out of that came bitterness and disdain where before America was revered. We were now considered bullies who would use our dominant power wherever we chose unilaterally.

Another is the political ineptness of the two parties who continue to create conflict over ideology rather than coming together to find ways to resolve important issues. As citizens we support one party and when it doesn't produce results we vote for the other, all the while stalemate continues and we flounder rudderless down the rapids.

I have a problem with his suggestions on what needs to be done for America to remain the dominate society. He minimizes the spread of Islam in Europe and around the world and he doesn't support doing anything to counter the unfair business practices primarily of China but other countries as well.

It is my firm belief that Islam with its Sharia law threatens to stifle human progress by dragging the world back 1300 years ago. The chaos they create around the world cannot be ignored but of course with Obama as President we are powerless to face up to the threat.

He berates the meager attempts by one House or another in Congress to penalize China for artificially inflating their currency creating an unfair advantage for American workers. Add to that the many ways they steal or manipulate Corporations to give their secrets plus ignoring copyright protection.

Many people are satisfied with low cost items found at Wall—Mart and the soaring stock market. These are the people who don't understand that American manufacturing is important and that those engaged in factory work should be able to earn satisfactory income. We tax manufacturing at the highest rate in the civilized world. I would start by cutting it in half. Secondly regulations that are unnecessary would be eliminated. Frivolous law suits would be curtailed. Unions would be directed to promote jobs not force companies to shut down. Place a tariff on all Chinese goods equivalent to overcome their manipulation of currency. All of the above to jump start manufacturing. If that wasn't sufficient I would go further. Remember good jobs paying good wages would provide income to be taxed plus those employed would not then be drawing down unemployment checks, using food stamps or be on welfare reducing the monetary drain on resources.

This book is worth reading as long as you don't swallow whole his statements.

Jack B. Walters
July 5, 2012

Seven killed in Afghanistan identified as US troops

This was the headline of an article in the 7/10/2012 edition of the Arizona Daily Star.

This occurred one day after donor nations meeting in Tokyo pledged $16 billion in aid.

If the bombing or suicide act was an isolated incident it could be chalked up to unfortunate but it isn't. Every day for weeks now I have read about continuing attacks on allied forces, sometimes by Afghans wearing uniforms and using weapons given to them by us. Is it any wonder how depressed our troops are after having to try to train natives never knowing when one of their recruits is going to turn on them?

Neither Obama nor Romney will withdraw so the bloodletting, misery and funding will continue without end unless the American people make their voices heard. This will not happen. Other people's children are doing the fighting and dying and they don't care about the burden they are placing on generations to come. They are not personally involved so they shrug it off.

Jack B. Walters
July 10, 2012

Deception of our elected officials

Having pondered this subject for some time now, I decided to attempt to put thoughts to paper about how the military/ industrial alliance has called the shots for over 65 years. I contend it started during the Korean War after the Chinese attacked us during the coldest part of the winter. Truman, out of concern for Russia, refused to allow General McArthur to attack the enemy North of the Yalu River. We had overwhelming superiority in air power but it was useless to him as he could not bomb the air bases or supply routes. Russia had attained nuclear status by then but was far behind our inventory. I believe Truman's fear was not justified. What bothered me the most was that he allowed the fighting and dying to continue without using our airpower effectively? We voted overwhelmingly for Eisenhower believing that he would finish the fight with victory. That did not happen as he did not consider it a priority.

During his eight years as President he kept the alliance under control. His warning to us as he was leaving office was to be aware of the alliance. His warning fell on deaf ears. During the campaign Kennedy kept referring to a "missile gap" inferring that Eisenhower had let Russia pull ahead. This was proven later to be false but I am sure had some effect on the election. To his credit Kennedy was successful in holding back the Joint Chiefs of Staff until his assassination. They had insisted on bombing Cuba back to the Stone Age and pushed for fighting troops in Vietnam. With his death there was no holding back. Lyndon Johnson, on a false premise that we had been attacked, turned loose the dogs of war. Vietnam never should have been fought. Millions killed and our country was thrown into deficit financing as Johnson insisted on fully funding the war together with his great society program. The protests started resulting in Johnson refusing to run for re-election.

After him came Nixon. He pretended to be reducing our troop levels but in fact for nearly every plane returning soldiers from Vietnam they had arrived with new soldiers. It was a farce. Americans finally had all they could take and took to the streets to protest in earnest which forced the government to stop.

The arms race went into high gear during the "Cold" war. Russia and the U.S. spent billions on delivery systems for nuclear weapons; bombers, missile sites and subs. Eventually Russia went broke and the Soviet Union broke apart. Our expenditures wreaked havoc on our economy as well but not to that extent. During these years under Reagan he broke the arms treaty that had prohibited missile defense systems. These programs were and still are extremely expensive.

President George H.W. Bush decided to go to war with Iraq after they had conquered Kuwait. Bush felt that Iraq might also decide to conquer Saudi Arabia, a country labeled as an ally. For the life of me I don't understand. They were the leader after all in 1973 when OPEC was formed and the price of oil was increased 10 fold overnight putting severe strain on the western countries.

President Clinton put Iraq in a tight position with sanctions and no-fly zones for the eight years of his presidency. He also used our Air Force in Bosnia and Kosovo when Europe was deemed unable to do the job. Then of course after 9/11/2001 the new President George Bush convinced Americans that we had to retaliate first against Afghanistan and then Iraq. Here we are 12 years later still fighting and dying in that part of the world having suffered many thousands of casualties and trillions of dollars spent. Obama has just approved four billion per year in aid for another ten years after we leave supposedly in 2014. We are similarly supporting Iraq. There is no end in sight.

The point I am trying to make is that as hard as we try to put a President or member of Congress in office to change course for the most part we have failed.

At the U of A book festival this Spring I purchased a great book entitled "Addicted to War" by Joel Andreas. It is done in cartoon style. Regardless, he makes the point very well that we are indeed addicted. One very good reason is jobs. The Defense Industry is protected from foreign competition and therefore the employees enjoy high earnings and benefits. The industry has very cleverly spread bits and pieces in nearly every state in the union which means at election time these people vote their paycheck. Politicians cannot safely speak about cutting back or they would not stand a chance of being elected. In this book he states there are over 100,000 companies providing the Pentagon with products and services. A few of the largest are; United Technologies, Textron, Northrup Grumman, Boeing, Raytheon, G.E., General Dynamics, Lockheed Martin and Halliburton. Further he states that our annual budget is larger than the next 36 countries combined, a full 36% of total global military spending. Nearing completion is a humongous carrier named after President Reagan at a cost of $1 trillion. It will have a crew of 5,000. Can you imagine the daily cost of a ship this large? For what it's worth in my opinion the day of the carrier is long gone. There are increasingly sophisticated missile systems coming on line that could destroy a carrier. Sure hope I am wrong on this.

I attended a very well done documentary last night entitled "Heist" "Who stole the American Dream". It all started with a document called the Powell Memorandum which was written in 1971. In it Mr. Powell strongly exhorted the Chamber and in particular big business to become active in the political process including lobbying. Powell became a Supreme Court Justice in 1969 being appointed by President Nixon. In 1978 there was a case called Boston vs. Bellotti. Powell was instrumental in overturning a Massachusetts's law restricting corporate contributions. Some claim this was the forerunner of the latest victory for business when the Court stated corporations were people which opened the flood gates of money during the current election process.

In the 70's there was a lot of anti-business actions taken by the Congress particularly under Carter. Agency after agency was created to put control over industry in particular. Regulations added greatly to the cost of doing business and severely hampered our competitiveness with products flooding in from overseas. I was fighting the good fight during those years and did lobbying myself, so I find I agree with the essence of the memorandum. What I disagree with totally is that the contributions have grown so excessive that the whole political system is out of control. It is common knowledge how much time elected officials spend raising funds for re-election. It cannot be denied that favors are granted in return. This is true of both parties. Full time lobbyists number over 30,000 in Washington alone.

I doubt if I will be able to make the point how different it is today compared to my era. As a Plant Manager my responsibility wasn't only to make a quality product at the lowest cost possible but to be a good citizen of the community and support it as best we could. The communities were better places because we were there. Fast forward to today, there is no consideration for communities, employees or anything else, only profit. To that end the companies have razed our cities by sending jobs overseas at an ever expanding rate. There is no consideration for the devastation left after they leave. What government can do is assure fair trade and take whatever steps are necessary to create good paying jobs for Americans. Should they try, the Chamber will oppose them but for the sake of working Americans, the effort must be made.

My title for this article was deception of our elected officials. We hear wonderful words but when push comes to shove they bail out and leave us floundering. They just don't care except for themselves.

Jack B. Walters
July 13, 2012

234

Rep. Bachmann's new McCarthyism deserves censure

This was the headline for your lead editorial column on 7/21/2012, which was from the Los Angeles Times.

They and you are wrong. I won't argue about Huma Abedin but it is common knowledge about the number of Muslims given positions in the Obama Administration. People associated with CAIR and other groups dedicated to the overthrow of Democracies like ours. All you need do is read your own newspaper to understand the worldwide assault of radicals to install Sharia law everywhere. To hide your head in the sand and ignore it is ludicrous. Finally a member of Congress is asking questions. Bring it into the light and see what can be discovered.

By the way, once again our illustrious Senator McCain has taken the wrong road.

> Jack B. Walters
> July 21, 2012

Offshoring and Repatriating U.S. Jobs

Last week the U.S. Senate voted down this bill by a vote of 56 for and 42 against. It needed 60 votes to pass. Senator's Kyl and McCain voted with the majority of Republicans to kill it.

The substance was to stop allowing companies from taking a business deduction for dismantling and sending a factory overseas and offering instead a 20% tax credit for expenses associated with bringing jobs back.

I am asking the editor to request why our Senators voted as they did and why the Republicans couldn't see the potential good from a bill like this. Corporations will be allowed to continue reducing their costs of outsourcing. What other country on earth does so little to protect jobs for their citizens.

The Republicans were given overwhelming majority in the House in 2010.

Nothing positive to create jobs has been accomplished in two years. Confusing isn't it.

Jack B. Walters
July 22, 2012

2016: Obama's America

A documentary film co-directed by Dinesh D'Souza and John Sullivan

They pose the question of where will we be if Obama wins a second term.

I went to see it today. There weren't more than 30 attendees and no young people. At the end those attending clapped their hands. It wasn't a joyous type of celebration due to the content of the film. I will be sending a copy of this article to my entire mailing list, over half of whom to this day are staunch supporters of Obama. Regardless, I am asking all to see this film, after all what should they be afraid of. If they think it is garbage, at least they will have shown enough interest to check it out. This film reminds me of Fahrenheit 911 a Michael Moore film which was a negative review of the presidency of George W. Bush. I saw that with my liberal friends at that time. I am specifically requesting they attend, if nothing else but to square the books.

This film follows Obama's life journey and points out the major persons who influenced his thoughts. Most were anti-colonialists or outright communists. They go to great lengths to prove their thesis; case in point, the strange decision to return the bust of Winston Churchill. They claim it was because of Churchill's earlier life as a colonialist of India and other countries. There are many names listed including his Kenyan born father who abandoned Barack at an early age. Much of the film includes scenes from places of interest including Hawaii, Indonesia and Kenya. They interview Obama's half-brother who lives in a shack in Kenya without any assistance from Barack which seems bizarre until you understand the difference in philosophy between them.

They refer to Obama's first book "Dreams from my Father". They contend he was influenced by what he knew about his own father but more importantly by his third father Frank Marshall Davis an avowed communist on the FBI register as someone to keep track of. Barack lived with him from age 9 to 18.

The ending suggests a bankrupt America which loses its standing in the International community and also weaker militarily so that we become vulnerable. He shows the entire Middle East as totally converted to Islam surrounding little Israel who will be left to die without American support. This is pretty scary stuff. Check it out for yourself.

Jack B. Walters
September 1, 2012

Who is the racist?

I am white. Four years ago I and millions of other whites voted for Barack Obama. I liked what he said.

Obama has not lived up to his promises. Almost everything he promised to do he didn't accomplish such as his pledge to make us energy independent in four years. He added $5 trillion to the debt when he said he would bring it down. His health care bill is an abomination which greatly adds to our debt and adds 15,000 IRS agents to track down those who are not enrolled in a private plan.

This time I will vote for Mitt Romney, a decent family man with a proven record of accomplishments and service. I told a Democratic friend and he said I was racist. I reject that statement.

Over 90% of blacks will vote for Obama in spite of his abysmal record. That is being racist.

Jack B. Walters
September 10, 2012

The Party is over
By; Mike Lofgren
How Republicans Went Crazy
Democrats Became Useless
And the Middle Class Got Shafted

I just happened to catch a Public TV program where Jim Lehrer was interviewing Mike Lofgren. Afterwards I ordered a copy of his book. Wow, he really takes the Republican Party apart and at the end gives the Democrats' a shot, just too even things out.

Since the early eighties until just recently he was a Republican working in various positions on Capitol Hill. He finally became fed up and just walked away. He writes in clear unmistakable language the problems he sees in the party. For those reading this who have agreed with me that Obama must go you will not enjoy reading this book. I must say I didn't either. I purchased it in the interest of fairness. We get carried away only reading articles and books that support our agenda and refuse to listen to the other point of view. Those of you who have not agreed with me should rush right out and buy a copy. You will be thrilled.

Most of you who have received articles from me in recent years know how I feel about our current president. You should also remember my complete disdain for the past president. In short it would appear that neither party nor president has performed as government should, in my opinion. That is why I register as an Independent except for a brief changeover so I could vote for Ron Paul in the primary. He was the only one who promised to bring our troops home from Afghanistan and the rest of the Middle East.

There are twelve chapters. He is most irritated by the tax policies slanted for the benefit of the richest among us, their drumbeat for using our armed forces as a tool instead of diplomacy (Senator's McCain and Lieberman are the chief proponents), the influence of the religious right and the incessant overextending our military machine, all of the above without regard to taking us down to financial ruin.

In the last chapter he provides thoughts on how to get our government under responsible control. The number one item is to stop the outrageous money being poured into both parties principally by Corporations who the Supreme Court has granted that they have the same rights as real people and can spend as they desire on campaigns. If you are paying attention at all you must realize how bizarre this is. Over $1billion has been raised for each presidential candidate alone, and similar amounts to all other candidates for office. With those funds comes leverage to pass legislation favoring the contributors, not the American people. The amount of time devoted to raising funds rather than enacting the countries business is outrageous. His solution is public funding of reasonable candidates with no money from individuals, corporations or unions. Shorten the election campaign to several months as other nations do. Perpetually running for office leaves little time to solve our problems. I proposed similar thoughts in my "Still Angry" book, but that is beside the point. You must agree that constant concentration on picking candidates and campaigning is out of control. The media, of course, love it for the revenue they receive.

I wonder who will be interested enough to check out this book?

Jack B. Walters
September 13, 2012

Letter to the editor 9/14/ 2012

I have waited several days before weighing in with my assessment of the destruction of our Embassy in Libya and the accelerating attacks on Embassies in the Middle East, not all of them American.

To hear Hillary and Obama apologizing for a film made by an Egyptian is disgraceful to me. We, as Americans, either believe in free speech or we don't. There is no half way point. If the Islamists get their way free speech and our Constitution will cease to exist, replaced by Sharia law which is reprehensible and the worst type of hate filled dictates.

The Middle East is a dangerous place made more so by our complicit removal of the strong men who had kept a lid on the radical Muslims. Our Congress is even now approving billions in armaments for Egypt and other Islamic nations all of whom are dedicated to the destruction of Israel. Our President has left them out in the cold to fend for themselves. This is outrageous and criminal in my opinion.

Jack B. Walters

Pakistan, Egypt, Libya Aid Cutoff

During the week ending September 21 the Senate voted on a bill to end financial aid to the countries listed above. The bill was defeated by a vote of 10 for and 81 against. Guess how our Senator's McCain and Kyl voted. Hooray for you, you guessed right. They voted to continue aid as if nothing had happened. Now they are home supposedly on a break until the elections are over with complete satisfaction of a job well done.

Should they take the time to ask constituents they would find to their amazement that 90% disagree with them? Oh, I know some of those funds find their way back to Raytheon and other armament producers. That still doesn't justify giving funds to countries who hate America and Americans. The Star will not allow me enough words to explain. If you are not aware, restating would be useless.

Jack B. Walters
September 23, 2012

The Fine Print
How big companies use "Plain English" to rob you blind
By David Cay Johnston

Mr. Johnston is a financial investigative reporter. This is his third book. The first two were "Perfectly Legal" and "Free lunch". He has appeared in a documentary and is often interviewed on news channels relative to financial matters. Several years ago I placed reviews of his books on my blog. It is jackbwalters.blogspot.com. In searching the Internet for reviews of his books he discovered mine. He was pleased enough to write to me. We kind of became pen pals. He lives in Rochester, N.Y., my sister lives in my home town of Lockport, N.Y. which is about 50 miles from Rochester. I try to visit her every year. For two years I was able to combine these visits with a drive to Rochester to have breakfast with David. He was kind enough to sign my copies. Since I am also an author, I gave him copies of my three books. He was complimentary but at the same time advised that they would never sell. He was correct. Over 90% were just given away to friends and family. His books on the other hand were best sellers. After those two years we were never able to co-ordinate my visits so we could get together. What with his writing and interviews he is just not available. I still treasure those two opportunities. He is doing a great service for America. If only those in power would read they might become more responsive and start the financial recovery of our country. You and I know that is not going to happen. They are too busy raising campaign funds to worry about actually doing something positive.

Now about this new book, if anything it was more depressing than the first two. In chapter after chapter he spells out the mismanagement of our tax dollars not only at the Federal level but also State. It was very hard to read. I could only take a chapter at a time. I would put it down and start again another day. The money being given to politicians is mind boggling and the largest given in return inflates the profits, particularly of the largest corporations by providing ways to hide profits so little or no taxes are paid. One issue happened in 2004. The corporations that had moved American jobs to China and elsewhere were required to pay 35% tax on profits but only when returned to America. The Congress in its wisdom granted them a special tax of 5%. The bill was called "the Jobs Creation Act of 2004". It was passed with 205 out of 221 Republicans and 75 of 199 Democrats.

The corporations brought home $312 Billion. While there was a promise of American jobs, nowhere in the bill did it specify nor was there any provision to monitor. In actual fact thousands were laid off. As an example Pfizer closed whole factories. The workforce at the end of 2004 was 115,000. By 2009 it was down to 75,000. Hewlett—Packard immediately fired 14,000 employees. Other industries did the same. Astonishing that such a disgrace could occur under the guise of helping American workers. Believe it or not in 2012 these same corporations have accumulated $1 Trillion in untaxed profits. I am well aware that consideration is being made to repeat this once again which will deny proper tax payments and destroy several hundred thousand more jobs. Once again it will be the Republican Party most in favor. Regardless of who becomes President, this will be approved. Keep in mind that all the while American manufacturers producing in America pay 35%. Can you not see how wrong this is?

There are specific chapters about abuses in pipe lines, railroads, waste removal, telecommunications, film production, etc. Each time he clearly states the facts which beg for correction.

His final chapter is entitled "Solutions". The most important concerns the 2010 Supreme Court decision to grant corporations unlimited expenditures to influence elections. He particularly chastises Chief Justice Roberts for giving them vast new rights. He mentions previous bad decisions by the Court such as the Dred Scott decision that stated that slaves were not persons protected by the Constitution. He pleads that the Congress take action to overturn or that new justices might reverse. Since the decision was 5 to 4 that could happen but in the meantime untold damage will have occurred to our election system.

I will end here by imploring others to read this and his other two books and do what you can to restore a Congress that truly cares about American workers.

Jack B. Walters
October 10, 2012

We Are No Longer a Christian Nation

Those words were said by President Obama in June 2007. Since that time he has said essentially the same thing by denying that America is a Christian nation. Sad to say, he just might be correct. There is a decided difference in America of today as compared to our early history right up to WWII.

From the history books I have read there can be no question that our leaders adhered to the Christian faith. There were numerous times when prayers were given asking for God's blessing. The God referred to was the Christian God not Allah or any other. In God we Trust is still just barely on our currency. All over Washington the buildings have inscriptions referring to God. Every State Constitution makes reference to God.

Jack B. Walters
November 2, 2012

1%
Twilight of the Elites
America after Meritocracy
By Christopher Hayes

I have a good friend who currently is of the opposite political persuasion. We banter back and forth. I share books and articles with him. He lent me his copy of this book. I have just finished reading. He will no doubt be astonished that I agree almost totally with this author. It has been my contention right along that those on the right and on the left are all dissatisfied with the current state of affairs. Where we should be collaborating, the powers that be are content with us battling back and forth while the Elite among us continue to enjoy outstanding wealth and privilege.

To start with a definition of meritocracy is required. I was going to quote my Webster Dictionary but it isn't even mentioned. Perhaps my copy is too old. The author's general definition is that those in the meritocracy are the cream of the crop, natural born leaders, and highly intelligent, hard charging persons regardless of sex or race. Some came to power from wealth or privilege. These are the people who generally make the decisions that affect all others in the world. This is not a bad thing as we want the best and brightest to make those critical decisions necessary to keep moving forward.

The problem as he and I see it is that in recent decades starting in the 1980's in America there has been a disconnect between these leaders and the rest of us. Without regard to the general prosperity of the average citizen, these Elite have made decisions that have had the direct effect of lowering our standard of living while increasing their wealth astronomically to where it is incomprehensible to even imagine. He spells this out in great detail.

He covers many different areas such as Wall Street, Congress, the Catholic Church, Corporate America and even Major League Baseball. All of these institutions have failed in their responsibility to citizens by ignoring our needs while protecting and enhancing their grip on power.

He points out the disastrous effect of the Supreme Court decision to allow Corporations to spend unlimited funds on political elections thereby assuring their continuing dominance regardless of which party is in the majority. All politicians are deeply indebted to those Elite who shower funds on their behalf.

On page 181 he quotes Thomas Paine on the importance of the proximity of politicians and those who elect them, "That the ELECTED might never form to themselves an interest separate from the ELECTORS, prudence will point out the propriety of having elections often, because as the ELECTED might by that means return and mix again with the general body of the ELECTORS in a few months, their fidelity to the public will be secured . . . . On this . . . . depends the STRENGHT OF GOVERNMENT, AND THE HAPPINESS OF THE GOVERNED."

The author doesn't mention the following but I wish too. The above has become meaningless as Congress has become a career instead of service. Something over 90% of Senators and Representatives are re-elected time after time. This in my opinion creates the distance between them and not being able to understand the lot of our citizens.

He is convinced as I am, that the ELITE are so far separated from the populous that they just don't care. As this separation intensifies sooner or later a backlash will occur as it does today in countries like Spain and Greece. To say it can't happen here is denying the reality. He points out how countries like Brazil have quietly and successfully closed the gap with the rich still getting richer but the rest catching up. It is possible to accomplish but we need the will to get it done.

Let us hope it does happen. This is a worthwhile book to read.

Jack B. Walters
October 17, 2012

Critique of election results 2012

All of the pundits are mouthing words to explain what happened this week with the overwhelming victory of President Obama over Romney. You, who know me, will not be surprised that I would want to add my own thoughts as well.

Romney's chance to win was compromised during the Primary process. The new Republican Party is so far right in its philosophy that he had to relinquish his more moderate positions to even be considered as their candidate. He was labeled a flip flopper as a result. During his contest with Obama he tried to be more attractive to moderates in the party or Independents but the label stuck. The fatal blow was the taping of him in a private meeting asking for contributions. He said "47% wouldn't vote for him" The inference was about lower income people including those receiving government checks. A good friend on Social Security took this to mean his comments referred to him personally.

This election could be the last opportunity to return to some type of fiscal sanity. Just today I read that Puerto Ricans had voted to accept Statehood. Those millions would automatically become Democrats. Should Obama be successful in granting citizenship to the millions of Latinos in the country illegally, those millions would also become instant Democrats. Even if the candidate in 2016 is not black, I believe blacks will continue to vote as a block as they have in recent times. People receiving unemployment benefits, welfare, Social Security disability insurance or food stamps will not bite the hand that feeds them. There are many other programs similar to the ones named that also provide checks for people who are not contributing to the general good of society. Unions can be counted on and the multitude of Federal employees who are enjoying the good life.

If the Republican Party is ever to become a viable alternative it must return to its original credo of fiscal conservatism not moral or "family" as it was transformed into back in the 70's. I watched it unfold while living in Iowa. It was during these years that evangelical Christians decided that the Republican Party was their best chance to influence government. Let me be clear, I never saw it written down or openly discussed but it was obvious to any observer. They started at the bottom with school boards, local offices of all kinds with the goal of infiltrating like-minded persons into government. As the years went by they incorporated their agenda into the process until it became the basis for the party platform. As I tried to convince family members to vote for Romney, I was told that no Republican will ever get their vote as long as their platform is anti-women's rights. The country is running out of white folks. Whites are no longer the majority of the population. There is nowhere to go but down. Unless the party finds a way to be inclusive to gays, Latinos, etc. it will decline to irrelevance. It is perceived now as the party of fat cats. By signing the Norquest "No tax increase" pledge they are seen as standing up for those at the top. Their attacks on Social Security and Medicare are not welcome by seniors or those hoping to have those benefits when they reach retirement age. Reducing death taxes to zero allows those with fortunes to pass their wealth onto following generations creating a permanent class of super-rich. We might as well be a monarchy; it amounts to the same thing.

I fear for the future of our country. With Obama installed I have no faith that the nightmare of annual trillion dollar deficits will be reduced. Now that the elections are over "thank God", the news media is drumming up how catastrophic the "fiscal cliff" will be if it goes into effect at the end of this year. Unemployment will sky-rocket and lay-offs will increase; the stock market goes into free fall, etc. Let me ask you, are you so selfish that you are not willing to pay your share today rather than leave it the coming generations to deal with. Is that the legacy we think is right to burden our children with? I say no. Funding for all wars must be paid for by us. If we don't like it then stop the fighting. It seems simple and straightforward to me.

There may be a snippet of co-operation between the Parties but I don't believe it will amount to anything other than providing sound bites for the Media to talk about. The deficits will continue unabated, the old wars will continue for two more years at a minimum, new wars will be started with Iran, if not some other country like Syria. Obama will continue catering to the Muslim community as he has done for the past four years, Israel will be left to fend for themselves, and China will continue taking our industry for their people by using the same strategy that has been so successful to date. We have already started the ongoing, never ending process of preparing for the next election, the Corporations will once again spend untold millions influencing Congress to do their bidding, As low as the approval rating of Congress gets the people still re-elect their Congress person or Senator. We could be energy independent but Obama will keep putting in road blocks to assure it doesn't happen, I will stop now with the above optimistic report.

Jack B. Walters
November 8, 2012

Just a Coincident

In just over one week after the re-election of Obama the Stock Market plunged, there were riots and massive strikes in Europe, Hamas in Palestine decided the time was ripe to start raining thousands of rockets into Israel,

A House Committee is finally allowed to see the real time video of the attack on our consulate in Benghazi. Obama, Clinton, Susan Rice, Petraeus knew that this was a coordinated attack. They all spoke only that it was provoked by a stupid video made by an Egyptian living in California. They were directed by the President in my opinion. Action could have been taken but wasn't.

Petraeus and Allen were found to have been guilty of being involved with women when they should have been taking care of their soldiers. It was known by the FBI last July but of course they wouldn't tell a President until after the election.

Keep watching, this is just Act I.

Jack B. Walters
November 16, 2012

It is time to pay the Piper

As a nation we cannot continue to go deeper in debt. I for one am willing to go over the cliff rather than keep adding to the curse of debt we are passing on to our children's children.

Let the Bush tax cut expire. Our country was coming out of deficits with the Clinton tax rates. There of course will be repercussions but it has to happen sometime, why not now?

Bring our troops home. Twelve years of trying has not changed the basics of Iraq or Afghanistan. Trillions wasted and precious lives lost. Face the reality that those people want to live the way they want. It is not Democracy nor will it ever be.

Stop giving Billions to those nations who hate us and hope for the day we collapse.

Stop the bleeding of the giveaway programs that are turning our people in to takers rather than givers.

Jack B. Walters
December 7, 2012

2013

2013

Listing in order by date;

American Women in Combat

I have waited since the announcement for reaction from the public in opposition to this decision. Nothing, therefore I will provide my own. I am 84 and of the WWII generation. In my world it was the man's responsibility to do the fighting and dying. We would not contemplate staying home and reading about the death or capture of American females. I realize my kind are old fashioned and out of step with the new world. So be it.

America today is willing to send men and now women into wars as long as they are someone else's children. How different it would be if their sons and now daughters were drafted and sent into harm's way. Would we still have soldiers dying in Afghanistan after 12 years of useless squandering of lives and Trillions of dollars? I think not.

Jack B. Walters
January 30, 2013

We are being taken for a ride again, stay alert

Most who pay any attention to the subject of illegal immigration know that in 1986 President Reagan granted amnesty to over 3 million immigrants who were in our country illegally. As kind and generous people we accepted with the assurance that steps would be taken to secure the border and that E-Verify would be mandatory for employers to use to determine the citizenship of employee prospects. A stab was made. Over the 23 intervening years an additional 12 million or so are known to be in America without proper documentation. They find ways to procure fake Social Security Cards, Drive's licenses, etc. with ease. No matter how many billions have been spent on border fences, border patrol agents or electronic surveillance they keep coming. They are only slowed down when our economy tanks, otherwise it is business as usual.

The bleeding hearts among us think that this is OK, the more the merrier. Most of these types have never seen the inside of a factory nor have any idea what it is like to do manual labor by the hour, day after day, year after year. There are Americans who do. These are the ones who are robbed of decent wages for performing these tasks. My constant theme is to create an environment to where good wages can be earned by those willing to work at something other than sitting in front of a computer.

Spending additional funds on fences, etc. are only wasted dollars, only done to con the American people into thinking they are serious. E-verify was never made mandatory. We, the citizens of Arizona tried. We voted for it several years ago. To my knowledge there have been no serious efforts on the part of our State officials to penalize employers. SB 1070, wow, how much slack have we received over this? How many dollars have we taxpayers spent taking it all the way to the Supreme Court? Have any of you read about someone being pulled over on suspicion of being here illegally? I haven't either.

What is happening now is a political reaction by Republicans to the defeat they endured in the last election when over 70% of Hispanics voted Democrat. In my naivety I want to think that American citizens who are Hispanic think as I do and all other American citizens regardless of race or ethnic background. I guess I am wrong. What does that say about our long term survival as a country?

Isn't it interesting how politicians change their mind when they deem it necessary? Do you remember when McCain and Kennedy proposed amnesty? I heard him ask the question, "What should we do with these people". He was deriding those of his own party who wanted them returned to their own countries. Then when he was running for President he wanted huge fences built to keep them from continuing to flood into our country. Mitt Romney softened his comments when he realized the Hispanic vote was against him. That didn't fool anyone. I predict that not one additional Hispanic voter will vote Republican next time. It is a futile gesture that will backfire on them. During the decades this farce has been going on the Democrats loved the new voters and the Republicans liked the cheap labor. Lobbyists, I am sure, pummeled anyone who was serious about control. President Obama is being taken to Court by a group of Border Patrol agents for issuing orders contrary to the legislation enacted from which they get their orders on how to perform their duties. Perhaps the Supreme Court will put an end to his Executive orders in question. I don't have much hope after witnessing their decisions on health care and political contributions by Corporations.

On a talk show program last evening the question was asked about how illegals would be treated the day after amnesty is granted. The answer was they would not be treated the same. I consider that baloney. Once the door is opened it will never be closed. We might as well annex Mexico and the rest of Central America into a larger country rather than continue this farce. They will continue to desecrate Arizona wilderness areas. For an avid hiker like me this is sacrilege.

I will only be convinced when I am assured that employment verification is in place and being monitored on a continuous serious basis. I don't mean decades from now, I mean now.

For whatever good it might do I intend to send this message to our elected officials. They can add it to the short stack of zealots like me and ignore as they usually do.

Jack B. Walters
February 2, 2013

HR325 Amendment
(This letter was sent to Senators McCain and Flake)

You owe it to the citizens of Arizona and all the rest of the States to explain why you voted yes to kill the amendment that would have stopped giving F-16 fighter jets and Abrams tanks to Egypt.

Ever since the US sponsored overthrow of President Mubarak the Muslim Brotherhood has created havoc in this country. President Morsi has compared Jews with apes and pigs. Those who rebelled initially for freedom have been denied, chaos is the current situation. The only country that these advanced weapons will be used against is Israel. The Republican Party is supposed to support Israel. The only reason to proceed with this give away is to promote jobs in the Defense Industry. If that is your reason why not give to anyone, how about Iran or N. Korea. I'm sure they could put these weapons to good use.

We, as a nation, are drowning in debt. You and others continue to talk about domestic programs such as Social Security and Medicare, all the while continuing to give billions to countries that basically dislike us intently. Just look at their voting records in the United Nations. They oppose us the majority of times.

You are concerned about upending relations. Let me state for the record, ever since President Carter got Begin and Sadat to shake hands it has cost America billions in aid to both countries, a great way for him to receive a Nobel Peace prize.

I am a stanch supporter of Israel. They are surrounded by those of the Muslim faith who hate them and will not stop until that country is destroyed. When that occurs, the rest of civilization will die along with them. President Obama lauds Islam continually. It had been my hope you would recognize the situation and do whatever you could to support Israel. You cannot begin to understand my disappointment with your latest vote.

Jack B. Walters
February 3, 2013

Mr. Doug Kreutz,
Bighorns Article in the Star 2/10/2013

I am writing as a private person who for two decades has been an avid hiker ever since I arrived in Tucson. The Catalina's being nearby is the range I hike most often. For many years the range has been closed to hikers during the prime hiking months to protect the Bighorns during lambing season. It has been obvious to me and others that they just were not there any longer.

In your second paragraph Jim Heffelfinger states that the last remnants of a native herd died out about a decade ago. He is a regional game specialist with the Arizona Game and Fish Department. I am outraged by this comment. For the department to deny hiking for a decade is unconscionable when they knew there was nothing to protect. I am asking you to send a copy of this letter to him asking for an explanation.

The Catalina's are surrounded by over one million people. Many enjoy hiking. Just visit the parking lot at Sabino Canyon any day of the week and you will see most spaces occupied. There are houses on the side and top. There are many fine trails for hiking. If introducing will have the effect of denying hiking experiences over extended periods of time and locations then I believe relocation should be done in other ranges less populated.

The other concern I have is mountain lions. In 2004 they were hunted and killed in the Sabino Canyon area. I was opposed to that then and want to register my opposition to a renewed killing spree. Fellow hikers know, as I do, that at least one lion has been sighted in the Canyon. I have heard that this is being contemplated. I would assume that after introduction of the Bighorns that an annual hunt would be conducted to remove these would be predators.

In the same day's news there was an article on page A11 about the "2013 Predator Masters Annual Hunt &Convention" in Las Cruces, N. M. This same group was invited to hunt for predators in the Globe, AZ area in February 2009. I wrote a letter of protest. It was published in the Star. I am attaching a copy of it and also two letters I wrote pertaining to the lion hunt in Sabino Canyon. The first was angry. The second was more reasoned. I am sharing with you to provide a different point of view.

You have written many articles about hiking. You have been an ardent supporter of the sport which is the reason I am writing this to you today.

Jack B. Walters
February 10, 2013

Big Horn Sheep re-introduction to the Catalina Range

In an article in today's Arizona Daily Star Columnist Tim Steller exposes what may be the ulterior motive for placing a herd of Bighorns in the Catalina's. That motive is hunting. This program will cost hundreds of thousands. We have read about how they plan to protect the sheep by having them wear collars and thereby find one who has died. Should the perpetrator be a mountain lion then a team will be dispatched to slay the offender. However providing hunting permits for humans to take their trophies they believe to be a great achievement. How nice for the hunters. Just think of it, no more long drives. Just kiss the wife and tell her you plan to return for lunch.

My main objection to this is that the Catalina's are surrounded by a million people. Thousands hike the myriad of great trails daily. These trails go to all areas including Pusch Ridge. Do they plan to deny access during hunting season as they have for decades lambing season? Remember they admitted banning hiking when they knew sheep were non-existent.

Leave the sheep where they are now and appear to be thriving. Use the money for some other useful purpose.

Jack B. Walters
July 7, 2013

Luke's Popular Air Show Canceled

The above was a front page article in The Arizona Republic 2/16/2013. The essence was that due to impending military budget cuts next month the show was cancelled.

This is the traditional response to budget cuts whether in the military or transportation or anything else. Do something that directly impacts the public. Not fixing potholes is the response those of us living in Tucson well understand.

An air show has a number of good things attributed to it; entertaining citizens, in particular children, showcasing the latest equipment, meeting military personnel and creating a positive relationship between citizens and the Air Force. By cancelling, the hope undoubtedly, will be a groundswell of public support to not cut funding. It, no doubt, will be successful. It always is. There are any number of cuts that could be made without decreasing military preparedness, known to many.

Shame on Brig. Gen. Rothstein and his superiors in Washington.

Jack B. Walters
February 18, 2013

Abel Emerging
A reconsideration of the Christian story for a sustainable world
By Ron Rude

Ron is leading an OLLI Course on Presidents and doing a fine job. He shared information on two books he has written. This book report is about his first book. He is a Lutheran Pastor and therefore a believer in God, Jesus Christ and all that entails, but he is far different from the norm in that he also accepts that the Universe has evolved over eons of time and that modern Homo sapiens emerged about 70,000 years ago.

This is a bold refutation of the standard beliefs of most who profess a belief in Christianity, those who proclaim without reservation that every word written in the Bible is irrefutable and true. This author proclaims the story of Adam and Eve is not an actual event but rather a way of expressing the unfolding of mankind. The title of the book relates to Abel as representing those humans who are givers, ready and willing to live frugally with respect for all living creatures, while Cain represents the takers, those who grab all they can for themselves without regard to the destruction of nature around them. He further states that the Cain's represent the majority of humans in positions of power including Christians.

In his introduction he proclaims that the Christian story needs to be re-considered. He bases this on the fact that the story is merely about Homo sapiens. He believes, as I do, that it needs to also include the wider community of life, from vegetation and animals to reptiles and bacteria, from landscapes and oceans to rivers and air. He believes, as I do, that Planet Earth is listing toward calamity and that humans are responsible. One comment he makes that I particularly agreed with was "Earth is humanities home (not a disposable way station on the road to an afterlife or heaven). He concludes this section by stating there is hope (but not in the short term).

He states that humans lived in harmony until about 6,000 to 10,000 years ago and that the relationship changed from living in harmony to one in which humans were regarded as special and that the rest of nature was here to be used and abused if necessary to serve their needs. He states that the Cain era started about 8,000 years ago. Here is where I want to intercede with my own thoughts. I believe the change occurred when formal religion took hold such as written in the Bible and the Koran. In the Bible it is clearly stated that man had dominion over all creatures on Earth. Further it promotes the afterlife as the goal, implying that life on Earth was only a passing step on the way to eternal life. It also refers to the end of the world as we know it and therefore it promotes the idea that the Earth will be destroyed anyway so use it to our hearts content as it doesn't matter.

At the present time it is estimated that over 30,000 species are being wiped out on an annual basis. Cain's culture has gained the upper hand. Entire peoples have been decimated, whole cultures laid waste. Traditions lost, family systems broken up and ecologies endangered to the brink of ruin. Like a cancer, Cain knows no boundaries and harbors no shame.

Cain's focus is on self, on immediate opportunities for exploitation, and an insatiable quest for more and more. Abel has regard for the water, soil and air, as well as respect for God, the whole community of life. In Chapter 5 the author does refer to the Cain philosophy that the world will be destroyed anyway giving humans license to do as they will without regard to the effect on nature. Chapter 10, he addresses the subject of afterlife. He states he believes in heaven, but only after we have lived a life that blesses life here. He states "If I can't be faithful with God's community of life on Earth, how will I be faithful with God's community of life in heaven"? He suggests that Cain's goal is to rule heaven also.

Chapter 11, Is there hope? In March 2008 the Southern Baptist Church declared that they had been too timid in the care of God's creation.

He finishes the book with hope that we will wake up in time to learn to live with nature as a partner rather than to be used. There are efforts well known of groups dedicated to this cause. We need to support them and hope for the best. That is the least we can do.

Jack B. Walters
March 2, 2013

Greg Byrne   April 3, 2013
U of Arizona Athletic Director

Dear Sir,

NOT GOOD ENOUGH

The controversy over the "jest" by referee director Ed Rush will not go away. The integrity of the entire sports program is under suspicion and will be until Mr. Rush is removed from his current position of authority.

As I have read, on two occasions he admonished the referees to go after the coaches and the second time with specific reference to our coach Sean Miller, a man Arizona fans hold in the highest regard. Over the years I have witnessed reprehensible conduct from coaches but not Mr. Miller. He is a complete gentleman, working in a volatile environment. To emphasize the seriousness of Mr. Rush's admonition he jokingly asked if he had to give a bonus for them to do their jobs. No one should suggest that it was a serious proposal.

The point I want to make from my own work experience as a factory manager is that a person in authority speaking to his subordinates, whether joking or serious, gets his point across of what he wants to be done. The subordinates then are duty bound to carry out his request. That's it, pure and simple. The call made on Miller was a direct result of this edict, not in a regular season game, but in a championship game with all that entails.

You need to understand that U of A fans take their sports seriously. We want to win or lose based on the skill of the players and coaches not on an arbitrary edict from on high. If you and the other Directors don't demand the removal of Mr. Rush then you are all abdicating your collective responsibilities.

Yours truly,
Jack B. Walters

One Down, One to go
(This was my second basketball officiating letter.
Ed Rush resigned. I was still not satisfied)

Ed Rush is gone, next to go should be Larry Scott the conference director for his comment that what Rush said was not a fire-able offense. He can no longer keep the confidence of the athletic directors, coaches and players if he truly cannot grasp the seriousness of the comments made by Mr. Rush to his officials.

Sports fans everywhere want integrity. They want the game to be decided by the players and coaches not an arbitrary edict from on high directed at the officials to go head hunting.

I read that the other Pac-12 directors had not commented. If that is correct, then shame on them too, as this incident wasn't just an Arizona concern but a concern for all the universities.

Jack B. Walters
March 5, 2013

My right knee

This is an update on the problem I have been having with my right knee. It began on 1/23/2013, the day after a strenuous hike. I was feeling strong that day and stayed right behind the guide. That is what I always had tried to do in my prime hiking years. Normally, of late, I hang back and just try to keep the rest in sight. Oftentimes I hike alone so as not to hold others up with my slow pace. At any rate I caused a problem with my right knee. Previously I had prided myself with the strength of my legs, in general, and of having no knee or foot problems. Don't suppose getting older has anything to do with what happened.

There was increasing swelling on the inside and a constant ache. I had difficulty sleeping as no matter how I laid the knee would keep me awake. On Feb 2nd I went to my Doctor. He ordered x-rays. They showed that the cartilage was OK, just slight arthritis. He gave me a 30 day supply of pain pills which helped. A couple of weeks later I noticed an increase in size of the varicose veins behind and to the side of the knee. I have had these distorted veins ever since my car accident in 1953. I began to think my thrombosis was the problem so I asked for an ultra sound check up. It came back negative. Evidently the Aspirin EC pills I take on a daily basis have cleared that up. I was relieved. When I ran out of pain pills I just continued on assuming it would gradually improve. It didn't. It continued to worsen. My hiking was almost totally stopped. Even playing golf with a cart caused me to not enjoy it much. I napped a lot but never felt rested.

I asked my Doctor to line me up with an Orthopedic Surgeon. He did and yesterday was my appointment. After a thorough checkup he did administer a Cortisone treatment. Somehow, I didn't watch, he was able not only to put in the drug but extracted fluid from the puffed up area. I felt instant relief. He had me purchase a knee brace to wear until the swelling is gone, do daily leg strengthening exercises and not hike for ten days.

I had a good night's sleep without pain and feel very positive that this problem is behind me. I will resume hiking as I feel it is important to my wellbeing but at my reduced pace that had been acceptable to me.

Just thought you might like to know. I am sending to family, hiking, golfing friends and others who were aware of my problem.

Jack Walters
March 22, 2013

Gay Marriage Controversy

The Supreme Court is considering whether it is discrimination against homosexuals by denying them the right of marriage.

The suit was brought after the Federal Court in California over ruled the will of the people who had voted against it. As I have read, blacks were overwhelmingly opposed.

Personally I can accept civil union but am opposed to marriage. With civil union, a couple, whether straight or gay can live together. I can even accept a Justice of the Peace or a ship's Captain. Marriage is a step too far. I have discussed this with two pastors. One said he favored marriage, the other said he would never participate in a gay wedding ceremony.

My question to you and anyone else who reads this article, is what happens to the minister who refuses to perform the ceremony? Can he or she be sued? Can the church to which he or she is the Pastor be found responsible and fined for inaction?

This is a far more important issue than the Catholic Church's objection to providing birth control to employees. Marriage is the most sacred of all rites.

In my opinion it was created for a man and a woman to join together and bring forth children in a loving union and thereby maintain the population.

Before you hit me with the response that gay couples are raising children, I have not stated that they cannot adopt.

So that is my simple short effort to state my opinion for whatever it might be worth.

Jack B. Walters
March 30, 2013

(Mr. Ron Rude sent me a booklet itemizing places in the Bible where same sex is mentioned. This was his attempt to reason with me.)

Dear Ron,   April 6, 2013

I appreciated receiving your little booklet about same gender unions. You saved me the trouble of searching through the Bible to find references about the subject. Actually I wouldn't have taken the time. I am satisfied with where I am on the subject and don't need to find a particular passage to help me decide. I come down on the side where I don't hate gay people but at the same time have become increasingly annoyed with the constant bombardment espousing the life style as if it were the normal thing and not the minority. We hear it daily in the news media, in plays, movies, TV shows and in the schools. I just wish they would live their lives quietly and leave me alone.

One of the men I most admired in this world turned out to be gay. He was a member of my church with a wife and two daughters. Out of the blue one day he announced that he was gay and had aids which shortly thereafter took his life. At the funeral his lover sat next to his wife and daughters. The church was packed as he was liked and admired by many. My church at the time was Plymouth Congregational in Des Moines, Iowa. We became known as an accepting church. I remember one Sunday as a Deacon during the service we were picketed by evangelicals from another church. I went outside with another Deacon to ask them to leave us alone. In actual fact I was so angry I let the other Deacon do the talking as I was afraid of what I might say. I only know that had they tried to enter the church I would have done my utmost to prevent it. They did depart.

Getting back to your book, at this point of my life I don't need to check the Bible to see if my thinking is correct. As you point out there are any number of places, particularly in the Old Testament where women are told to stay in their place, slaves are told to obey their masters and fathers are told to kill their sons if they disobey. I have never agreed with any of that. In my readings I have looked for what would help me to give direction on how to live a good life. As I said in my article "We are all God's Children", I don't try to state that I have lead a perfect life but that I have tried.

There is no doubt in my mind that they will prevail in attaining the right of marriage but not in a church I am attending as I will leave before that happens. I am sending your book to a young minister like yourself who I admire greatly and who is struggling with this issue as you have done.

Sincerely yours,

Another Con Job

In 1986, when Reagan was president, legislation was passed granting citizenship to three million illegal immigrants. We were assured that sufficient controls were being put in place to keep this from repeating, including workplace controls called E-verify.

Now over twelve million will be granted citizenship and E-verify will be phased in over five years. Give me a break. Can they really believe that five years must pass before enacting controls sufficient to convince employers to not hire persons here illegally?

Billions to be spent on border security. What a joke. There is not now nor has there ever been a serious commitment to secure the border. This is just to placate citizens into believing that all will be well.

We fell for it then and most will again now.

Anyone against this bill is labeled racist. How sad that most are cowed into silence because of this accusation.

Jack B. Walters
April 21, 2013

Islam

Once again I feel compelled to share my thoughts about Islam and the danger adherents to the faith present to the world community. I understand there are over 1.4 billion Muslims today. I recently sent out comments about the religion made by Winston Churchill 100 years ago. His analysis was right on, in my opinion. His main point being that strict adherence meant continuing slavery for women and girls. I have read many books on this subject which have convinced me of the evil this "religion" continues to do on a daily basis.

There is a difference today from years past. This was pointed out to me in reading "The Looming Tower" by Lawrence Wright. He details the beginning of Al-Qaeda in 1947 by an Egyptian and how it really took hold with Osama bin Laden while in Afghanistan which led directly to the 9/11 event we are all so familiar about.

People like me are labeled as Islamaphobic. We supposedly see a radical Muslim hiding behind every tree waiting to pounce. I have read that 10% of Muslims could be regarded as radical. Radical meaning they are ready and willing to commit havoc with non-believers wherever found. The math is simple, it means 140,000,000. It seems to me that this could be considered serious, but, of course, what do I know?

My continuing frustration is with our government and the news media, neither of which will come right out and state that a problem exists with Islam.

I include George Bush in my condemnation. After 9/11 he proclaimed that Islam was a peaceful religion. He, his father and the whole Bush clan have been in bed with the Saudi Arabia princes for decades. Do any of you remember how Bush allowed the many members of the bin Laden family to be flown out of the country all the while the airlines were shut down for the rest of us. As an aside, I always find it amusing that these privileged Muslims enjoy living in our decadent country.

As to our current president, he has extolled the greatness of Islam starting with his Cairo Speech shortly after becoming president. It is my firm belief that he has required our intelligence agencies and the armed forces to not even mention that an incident was committed by a Muslim. The Fort Hood massacre was labeled a work place dispute. How outrageous is this? While killing the soldiers he shouted "Allah Akbar". It has been three years and the Major has not been tried as yet while receiving first rate medical treatment and still earning his salary. This should have been handled with dispatch but that is not how our government works today.

It is impossible to read a newspaper and not read of some atrocity committed in the name of Mohammed somewhere in the world. Adherents are on an accelerated campaign to convert the whole world to their belief system. All the while Obama tries to cover it up. He blamed the Benghazi episode on a video, when it was clearly an organized assault, not a spontaneous event. After all this time including Senate hearings and news media discussion the truth has not come out.

The latest is the terrible bombing in Boston by two Muslim young men. The elder spent six months in Southern Russia where the Chechnya Muslims live. As I understand it he was admitted to our country as an immigrant, given welfare and other aid. I wonder how much it would cost to travel to Russia and stay for that length of time. Something doesn't make sense. Our security was warned by Russia that he was a radical Muslim. I believe for political correctness that warning was ignored.

Another point worth mentioning is the tremendous cost. I cannot even contemplate the loss as a result of shutting down the entire city for a day. These two Muslim fanatics have shown how devastating an action like they took can be to America. I have no doubt others will follow in their footsteps. Not to disparage our security forces, who put their lives on the line for us, but what I saw was overwhelming forces committed particularly when it was known he was in the boat. There were hundreds of police officers at the scene.

Like the Fort Hood incident this young man will be in custody for years while the investigation goes on trying to prove him guilty at a cost of millions. He will be referred to as alleged bomber. Would sure be wrong to convict him without a trial, wouldn't it?

My main purpose in putting these words to paper is to alert you to the threat to America by Muslim terrorists who will continue to punish America for our presence in Muslim countries. The odd thing is my agreement with them about this issue. Bush's wars which are now Obamas were and still are the wrong wars for us to fight. For a fraction of the cost we could be energy independent. No one can ever convince me that those wars were not started by our addition to the oil in the Middle East.

Our travail is just beginning.

Jack B. Walters
April 30, 2013

Benghazi Hearing-May 8, 2013

I learned about the hearing in which three high ranking officials were to testify about the attack on our Embassy. I checked C-Span and the other news channels. Only Fox considered it important. I caught it just as it began. I was complimentary that they would not interrupt the testimony until, lo and behold they did. The commentator even apologized stating they had to pay their bills. I then went to my computer where I found it being broadcast by Public Television and watched uninterrupted until it ended. I spent at least six hours of my day. Of the people I will be sending this to, I would be willing to bet that none of them did as I did.

My long standing opinion on the subject did not change. What it did was confirm for me the outrageous conduct of the Obama government to not react in a prompt fashion to mobilize forces to come to the defense of our people and then when it was over to falsely claim that it wasn't an attack by Islamists but only Muslims congregating to protest a video, implying that it was really our fault. Obama, Clinton, Rice and Petraeus apologized over and over including Obama's speech to the United Nations a week later.

These three (whistle blowers) were appalled and spoke out, effectively ending their careers.

Eric Nordstrom had been the Regional Security Officer posted to Libya after the war. His testimony related to his repeated attempts to beef up security. As it turned out security forces were dramatically reduced instead.

Gregory Hicks, the Deputy Chief-Tripoli was in Tripoli. He attempted to get reinforcements to Benghazi. The Colonel in charge received a "stand down" order. No knowledge of the name of the person who gave that order, or more importantly the person in the Pentagon or State Dept. The committee chair Representative Darrell Issa has pledged to continue searching for the truth. We can only hope he does. This outrage cannot be allowed to stand. Mr. Hicks clearly confirmed it was a terrorist attack by a group called Ansar el-Sharia. The Libyan President also confirmed who the attackers were. He was contradicted by Susan Rice's appearance on five Sunday news programs when she stated that the attack was brought on by a mob angry at the video.

Mark Thompson was the Acting Deputy Assistant Secretary in the State Department with responsibility for anti-terrorism teams called FEST (foreign emergency support teams). He tried many times to receive approval to deploy a team. He was denied. Statements were made that it was too dangerous or they couldn't get there in time. How outrageous is that? What is the use of training military personnel to intercede when needed? They could have been called back at any time once sent. The fighting in Benghazi lasted over six hours. They might have arrived in time to save lives or at the very least exert deadly force against the perpetrators.

It has been proven that the assessment of the intelligence memo was re-written to exclude all comments relating to terrorists, at the direction of the State Department, which to me means Hillary Clinton. She and the rest continued to blame the attack on the video. As an aside I doubt if any of you have ever seen it, I did. It was available as a trailer of a movie. There is no movie that anyone has ever been able to find. It is 14 minutes long and the dumbest thing I've ever watched. Comical, not something that should generate hatred just disgust.

On the positive side, watching and listening to these three dedicated public servants was heartwarming to me. It rekindled my faith that there are great Americans working on our behalf all thru the government. They were very emotional as they recalled the events and at times showed anger at not being allowed to do their jobs as they were trained to do.

I can only hope you are as interested as I am in finally learning the facts of who made those fateful decisions that night and who decided to keep the truth from the American people. I will continue to follow this process to the end.

Jack B. Walters
May 9, 2013

What I believe about Islam

Muslims who live by the tenets of their faith believe they are superior to all other people who are not believers of Islam. Wherever they are in the majority they exert their power over all others. People who are Christians or Jews have been forced to leave until there are very few remaining in places like Iran, Saudi Arabia, Afghanistan, Iraq, Libya, Egypt and Turkey. For the most part those of the Jewish faith have fled to Israel. How convenient to have them so concentrated that at the right moment they can be annihilated which has been the goal since this religion was created 1,300 years ago. Just this morning in the Star was an article about students in Egypt turning in their teacher for supposedly anti-Muslim statements. She was arrested and will stand trial for blaspheme. There is no freedom of speech when Islam rules.

Jack B. Walters
May 11, 2013

Another women's issue

I find it tragic that the news media and all Americans can be so appalled at the imprisonment of those three unfortunate young girls in Cleveland but don't care a whit about the many millions of women and girls who are living as virtual slaves on a daily basis all over the world because they are living under the Muslim culture. Where Islam is dominant, they are forced to wear burkas and must obey their male relatives on penalty of beatings or death. There is no recourse for them by the legal systems.

When will, particularly the women of America, decide that this is of sufficient importance to take on as an issue, the same way they have been fighting for women's rights for a century in America? They cannot afford to wait for the men to take issue except for a few like me.

Jack B. Walters
May 11, 2013

Obama lashes out over Benghazi "sideshow"

This was the headline for an article in the 5/14/2013 edition of the Arizona Daily Star. There is truth in it; The Republican Party advocates will take every advantage to score political points. They have many opportunities today with the IRS being discovered giving special reviews of applications for tax free status of any group supporting the tea party. Also for two months in 2012 the government taped phone calls of Associated Press reporters ostensibly to find White House leaks of terrorist information.

Referring to my main concern Benghazi, I have been watching news broadcasts on different channels and to date I have been disappointed with the questions asked. They approach. They skirt around it. They imply but don't have the intestinal fortitude to come right out and state the truth. The Republican Congress is clawing their way up step by step looking for scapegoats. The process will continue unabated day after day, week after week, month after month; filling the news channels with content while leaving us waiting for the truth.

The truth, in my opinion, is that Obama was willing to sacrifice the Americans in the Embassy and then deliberately cover it up with the blatant lie that the attack was the result of the video, when clearly the intelligence community knew and reported that an Islamic group was attacking the Embassy. Hillary was told at 2:00 A.M. by Hicks. The next day she flatly stated it was a disgusting video which the American government had nothing to do with. She apologized all over the place instead of condemning the Islamic terrorists. I was revolted then and my revulsion continues unabated.

Am I the only one to recognize that Obama has and will continue to deny that Islam has anything to do with attacks on Americans or blame Islam for the many atrocities occurring on a daily basis everywhere in the world today.

All the aircraft carriers in the world will be useless if we don't have the resolve to fight back when required. With Obama at the helm we are defenseless.

Jack B. Walters
May 14, 2013

The Chicken Trail
Following Workers, Migrants and Corporations across the Americas
By Kathleen C. Schwartzman

I offer my complements for an outstanding overview of these most complex issues. She did a great deal of research, included many sources and made personal trips to processing plants in the USA as well as Mexico. She talked with Mexican farmers, illegal immigrants and union organizers.

She chose the radical changes in production of Chicken as a perfect example of the effect it had on labor in this country and loss of the family farm in Mexico which led inexorably in the increase of illegal immigrants to America.

She is very careful in not wanting her book to become political. She tries to state the facts and let them speak for themselves. I, on the other hand enjoy jumping in and calling a spade a spade so I am going to write this review from what I gleaned after reading.

Chicken processing advanced rapidly in the 90's impelled by innovation and technology. The largest plants are located in N.C., Alabama, Georgia, Arkansas and Mississippi. The workers were black for the most part. Chicken processing as well as manufacturing in general made great strides in the South due to the anti-union sentiment. The States were all right to work States. As the processes sped up there were increased injuries and fatigue resulting in the attempt to establish unions. The companies exhibited ingenuity in finding ways to avoid including going bankrupt and re-opening with a new name and firing all employees. The Company officers decided to replace with immigrants from Mexico and other countries. They advertised, paid bonuses, provided false papers, etc. No executive was ever found guilty of these most obvious offenses. In the meantime the black unemployment rate doubled. The new undocumented employees didn't complain about wages, working conditions, nor did they report injuries, all out of fear of being deported. I refer to this as the South discovering a new group of people to exploit as they did with the blacks as slaves many years ago.

While this was going on NAFTA made its mark in Mexico. By 2008 all tariffs were removed. Millions of farm families, who had subsisted, albeit poorly, were no longer able to support themselves. Not only Chicken but corn and grains in general. The highly subsidized agriculture in America was too great for them to compete with and so the great migration sped up in the 90's continuing today. Many would have stayed in their own country if they could have. We must add that the Mexican government leaders allowed this to happen impoverishing the countryside without concern. They should be held to account for allowing this to happen. Exporting young men relieved the need to provide employment, with the added benefit of Billions returned each year in support of families left behind. I know that other nations have protected their farmers such as Europe and Japan. I would also like to add my own comments about how American subsidies to agriculture benefited the largest farms effectively driving off the family farmer. I saw this in person the 23 years I lived in Iowa.

As far as I can see the new discussion in Congress about changing immigration laws will not address any of these issues. The Corporate Giants including Monsanto will still dictate policy and the little people; Americans and Mexicans alike will be used to their benefit. Just look at the recent farm bill. The farm bill should be used to encourage family farms not mega farms owned by the rich but worked by those who once had owned farms themselves.

Jack B. Walters
June 13, 2013

(Published in the Arizona Daily Star on 7/8/2013)

Thanks to the leadership of the gang of eight, John McCain and Jeff Flake we will have 40,000 border patrol agents, miles of fencing and drones. That should be enough to protect us from the Mexican people coming across. We only have 37,000 troops in S. Korea. They have done a wonderful job keeping out the million or more N. Korean troops from entering S. Korea. It appears to me that Mexicans are more feared than N. Koreans. The only difference is once they enter our country then they will be granted citizenship. I don't believe that option is available in Korea.

A thousand page bill costing $46 Billion. Kind of makes you proud that these great Arizona men have found a solution, doesn't it? Now if only the House Republicans join in, victory is at hand.

(In case you don't understand this is meant as sarcasm.)

Documentary Film
Dirty Wars by Investigative reporter Jeremy Scahill

I went to see this new film at the Loft Theatre last night. Mr. Scahill explores how our government has grown increasingly dependent on secret fighting. He traces the rise of the Joint Special Operations Command. These people are invisible operating under the direction of the White House. They, together with the ever expanding use of drones have drastically changed the rules of engagement.

It would appear that no matter how many enemies are killed, more rise up to take their place, clearly a scenario without a resolution.

In my opinion the only reasonable course for us to take is an orderly removal of our military from the entire Middle East. Nothing we have done nor could we do, can have any long lasting positive results. We are dealing with a culture that espouses violence as the way to resolve disagreements in their religious beliefs.

Do I think we will change course, of course not. Other than myself there were two other couples in the theatre. That tells me the lack of concern of the general public.

Jack B. Walters
July 2, 2013

The following letter was my response to an editorial column written by Leonard J. Pitts Jr. The title was "It's clear what stalked Trayvon down that night".

Dear Sir,   July 16, 2013

I only write to you after reading one of your columns where you write as a man of color rather than an open minded journalist. This one qualifies.

I'm not commenting on the substance only one issue. You referred to yourself as an African-American. I can't tell you how offensive that is to me. I really admired Herman Cain. He said he was an American whose skin happened to be black. I believe that the distinction you use is meant to separate you from Americans, who in your opinion are white and therefor racist.

With the circulation your columns reach if you would refer to yourself as American you might make a difference in people's attitudes black and white alike. Until we all join together as Americans the disharmony and suspicions will continue to the end of time.

I will look forward to seeing this change.

Jack B. Walters

Epilogue

I can't help myself. I can't just quit and give up. I must continue my useless effort of trying to wake up Americans to the perils that await if we do not band together to reverse the disastrous path our "leaders" have been taking us down ever since the assassination of John and then Bobby Kennedy. Since these brave and resolute men were murdered we have had a succession of self-serving people. I say people because I include women as well as men in my condemnation. They, Republicans and Democrats alike, serve the wants and direction of the elite without regard to either our people's needs or the world in general. We have witnessed a steady decline in the middle class to where we are left with the super-rich and the lower classes who exist on the largess of government programs designed, in my opinion, to keep them satisfied enough to not care about the deterioration of our once great nation.

This, my latest attempt, continues the writings I started in 2003, the year I finally acquired a computer giving me the ability to put words to paper. The Last Angry Man covered 2003 to 2006. Still Angry continued into 2010. This one carries into 2013. After this, who knows, I think it depends more upon my lifespan rather than declining interest.

I liken my writings to the efforts of the Pied piper and Paul Revere. I keep sending warnings of danger but no one it seems cares enough to follow my lead. That is too bad. I won't be around to see the end but will live long enough to hopefully see the people band together to start restoring America to the great country it once was.

I sincerely hope you found the articles meaningful and worthy of reading and sharing with others. That is the only way my hopes and dreams for my country can be accomplished.